Jennie Ozog

Jan' 04

ALSO BY KAY ALLENBAUGH

Chocolate for a Woman's Soul

Chocolate for a Woman's Heart

Chocolate for a Lover's Heart

Chocolate for a Mother's Heart

77 STORIES OF INSPIRATION

TO LIFT YOUR HEART

AND SOOTHE YOUR SOUL

A FIRESIDE BOOK
Published by Simon & Schuster

CHOCOLATE
for a
WOMAN'S
SPIRIT

KAY ALLENBAUGH

FIRESIDE
Rockefeller Center
1230 Avenue of the Americas
New York, NY 10020

FIRESIDE and colophon are registered trademarks
of Simon & Schuster, Inc.
Designed by Bonni Leon

Manufactured in the United States of America

3   5   7   9   10   8   6   4   2

Library of Congress Cataloging-in-Publication Data

Chocolate for a woman's spirit : 77 stories of inspiration to lift your heart
and soothe your soul / [compiled by] Kay Allenbaugh.
p.   cm.
1. Women—Religious life.   I. Allenbaugh, Kay.
BL625.7.C4667   1999
291.4'32—dc21   99-41727
CIP

ISBN 0-684-84897-X

This book is dedicated to spirit-filled women everywhere

who celebrate their ability to be strong,

intuitive, nurturing, powerful, playful,

witty, and wise—all at once.

CONTENTS

III
SPIRITKEEPERS

IV
THE POWER WITHIN

V

THINKING YOUNG AGAIN

VI

POSITIVELY INTUITIVE

VII
WAKE-UP CALLS

VIII
BOUNCING BACK

IX

CREATING ABUNDANCE

X

AGING WISELY

XI
BETTER THAN LAUGHING GAS

INTRODUCTION

*S*tories help us to learn about ourselves and make
discoveries that add meaning and depth to our life journey. As the creator of the *Chocolate* series, I've found
that stories play an especially profound role in the lives of
women.

The unforgettable true stories in *Chocolate for a Woman's Spirit*
honor and celebrate a woman's special ability to get quiet inside
and seek the universal truths in her spirit-filled life. Best-selling
authors, columnists, motivational speakers, and spiritual seekers
share stories that include being in the presence of angels, experiencing grace when it's least expected, and learning to trust our
intuition—God's gift to women. We find Spirit filling these
pages in an expansive way, as women think young again, become
spiritkeepers, create an abundant life, find love's riches, and
choose to age wisely. I'm quite convinced that Spirit has a sense
of humor, too. Just as you'll laugh when you learn how one
storyteller discovered how to really say *No,* you'll also be exhila-
rated as you read about a woman symbolically soaring through
her fears as she puts her trust in God, grabs hold of a rope, and
swings joyfully out over a large body of water.

The *Chocolate for Women* series of books has been, and continues to be, a divinely inspired project. I call it a "God job." In my
own life, every time I forget who's in charge, I fear my next step.
But when I remember *Chocolate* was created with His intention,
my faith increases and I relax into the joy and honor of being allowed to share these true-life spirit-filled tales with you. With

each success comes new challenges. My own spiritual journey has become one of awe as I discover that the quieter I get, the easier it is to listen. And the more I can hear that small, still voice speaking to me, the easier it is to get my ego out of the way—to let go and let God. The journey has been joyful, sometimes frightening, yet always rich.

As you read these stories and seek to apply their messages in your own life, I hope you'll be divinely inspired to take your own next step, especially if you're at a crossroads or are facing new challenges and opportunities. May the power of these heavenly stories heal your spirit and move you forward on your unique path—with a sense of humor and a sense of wonder. And may these stories inspire you to make the choices in your life that bring you the most peace of mind. By so doing, you'll know you're walking hand in hand with spirit.

I
THE FORCE IS
WITH YOU

"We must free ourselves to be filled by God.
Even God cannot fill what is full."

<small>MOTHER TERESA</small>

LOVE AT FIRST SIGHT

Many years ago, my uncle owned a restaurant at a small airport in Illinois. My mother was the assistant manager, and I was the hostess. One afternoon, my mother and I went to a diner for lunch. Our waitress, Debbie, was so sweet that we took an immediate liking to her, and my mother offered her a job at my uncle's restaurant on the spot. Debbie accepted.

We invited her to our home for dinner that evening and during our conversations with her, we learned that she had never married and that she had no boyfriend. She told us that five years before while on a flight back east, she met "her pilot" and that it was love at first sight.

She had been very nervous as she was boarding the plane and the pilot was standing in the doorway greeting passengers. He must have noticed how afraid of flying she seemed, and he struck up a conversation with her. They spoke less than ten minutes, and he assured her he would fly her safely to her destination. She told us it was love at first sight, and we told her there was no such thing. Although she never saw her pilot again, she never forgot the feeling she had in her heart when their eyes met.

Mother and I had a plan. Since she was so in love with her pilot, we decided to fix her up with one of the many single pilots that came into the restaurant to eat in between flights. We approached John, one of the pilots, and told him about Debbie. He agreed to meet her for a dinner date on one of his nights off.

We sat him at a nice table with candlelight and fresh flowers.

When Debbie arrived, we walked her to the table to introduce her to her date. As we approached, Debbie stopped dead in her tracks, tears welled up in her eyes, her hand went to her heart, and though I couldn't believe what I was hearing, she said, "My pilot, it's my pilot!" He stood dumbstruck and embraced her.

We later learned that he, too, had fallen in love with "his passenger" five years ago on that flight back east.

The last we heard from Debbie was in a letter from Guam. When people tell me there is no such thing as love at first sight, I tell them this story and show them the photo Debbie enclosed with her letter, a photo of her family—her husband, John, in his pilot's uniform and their two beautiful daughters.

KIM CHAMPION

IN SAFEKEEPING

Having lived and traveled through Central America for two years, I considered myself bus savvy. I knew all the schedules and times. I also knew better than to travel at night or take an unfamiliar route. So one night, when the bus I was riding broke down three times before we boarded another, which deposited everyone in the capital well after dark, I figured the gods were against me. I cried and pleaded with the driver not to leave me there alone, in a location totally unfamiliar to me, but he laughed like someone sick of American tourists and swiftly drove off into the pitch-blackness.

The few streetlights sported empty sockets from which the bulbs had been pilfered, and the only human presence seemed to be a couple reeking of liquor, asleep—or maybe dead! My imagination spiraled. *Where could the other passengers have gone to so quickly?* I wondered. Every headline, every story of women found raped, beaten, or dead in an empty alley seemed to reverberate from the hollows of broken windows and stripped cars, and propelled me to the signposts on the street corners. I had to figure out where I was.

Eight blocks later, I located two cross-street signs and plotted a path in my mind. A right turn at the next corner would lead me down a long street, through a tunnel, and into a park that I'd walked in often and knew would be populated even late at night. So began my long march toward safety.

One block before the tunnel, a man staggered out of a deserted building behind the only functioning streetlight and came right at me. He put one hand on my left arm and another in my hair, caressing it, pulling it. "You are beautiful," he slurred with his face pressed against mine, and I could smell the booze and the weeks of not bathing. "Tell me where you're going and I'll walk you there," he insisted, mocking me, still holding tightly to my arm. Not wanting to challenge or engage him by speaking or looking directly at him, I sized up his shadow on the wall. Not a big man, but nonetheless larger than I, and I knew at that moment, with absolute certainty, that he would attack me the minute I entered the confines of the tunnel that loomed before us.

Just then I heard another set of footsteps fall in behind me. Knowing attacks such as the one planned for me usually involve more than one person, I should have been terrified. And yet the minute I heard those footsteps, a sense of calm as palpable as the drunk man's groping hands descended upon me. As sure as I was two seconds ago that this drunkard would attack me in the tunnel, I was now equally certain that I would be safe. I glanced again at the wall to see the shadow of my savior, the owner of the second set of footsteps falling so close behind me, the one who would keep me safe.

No one was there. And yet the footsteps rang out, loud and piercing in the quiet night, reassuring me with each echo that I would not be harmed.

As I had predicted, when we reached the tunnel the drunk man lunged toward me, wrapping his hands around my neck and propelling me forward. But just as quickly he released me, and I stumbled backward as the force with which he was ripped from my body reversed my direction. I turned just long enough to see him fly through the air and land near the gutter on the other side of the street. No one else was there.

I made it safely through the tunnel that night. Now, whenever I'm afraid, I remember that night in Central America when I started out thinking the gods were against me. In the end, I knew they had been behind me the whole time. One night I heard their footsteps; I felt their force. And I have never been alone again.

ELLEN URBANI HILTEBRAND

> *"Nobody lives well who is not spiritually well."*
> JOAN TIMMERMAN

A (HEAVENLY)
CONVERSATION

T he books were piled up as they always were on
a Sunday night, and I sat down, hesitantly opened
a notebook, and reluctantly opened my mind. The
other half of my doom room was unoccupied, fortunately
—the mere presence of my roommate would have provided
a happy excuse for procrastination. I closed my eyes and
reached for a random book from the gigantic pile—religion. Well, at least this one is fairly interesting, I thought, and
dove in.

The church bells chimed hourly—once, twice. The CD
changer on my stereo became exhausted, and friends tried in
vain to distract me; still I read on. Page after page of theology
turned in front of me, managing to hold my attention, until suddenly my head began dropping . . . drop, drop onto my pillow,
and my eyes closed and I fell asleep, dreaming . . .

I sat in a large, airy, and delicate light blue room in a cushy
white beanbag chair. A woman dressed in a white sweat suit sat
opposite me in the same kind of chair. She had blond hair (California Sunshine brand), brown eyes, and a witty mouth. "Hi," I

said because she seemed so familiar to me, yet I couldn't place her.

Suddenly a thought hit me with the power and velocity of a bungee jump. All the pale colors, the serene atmosphere around me—could I be. . . ? Could she be. . . ? An idea came to me as if I were whispered the secret. *Omigod. Am I dead? And is this heaven? I expected it to be slightly more populated . . . How did it happen? Crossing the road to the dining hall? An overload of homework assignments?* I bit my tongue, thinking maybe I wasn't in the proper place for wisecracks.

"Are you God? Oh, my God. So, I'm dead," I repeated, just so I might convince myself. "I'm dead, in heaven, in a beanbag chair. And you're God. No kidding. I expected—"

"A guy," cut in God with an untraceable accent and a sigh. "Wouldn't you know? It seems to be the general idea. Actually, there's not much of a gender thing here. What's nice is that we can get up in the morning and just decide what we want to look like for the day. It's almost like changing clothes. You really get to know a person inside that way, because you can't pay attention to the outside." God crossed her legs neatly at the ankles.

"And you made it, the world and everything?" I inquired.

"Well, yes—no manuscript is without its typos, hmmm?" Another sigh escaped her red lips.

"No, no, it's not all that bad," I reassured God.

"It's hard for us all, just on a different scale," explained God patiently. "Your daily grind—work, school, friends—that's hard for you. Creation, keeping up on this place—those are my problems."

Well, I mused with a sense of smugness, *even God doesn't have it easy.* And then I hoped God couldn't read minds. "It seems pointless and for nothing most of the time," I told her. "I don't know what good I'm doing for the world or for myself by going through every day doing all of these mundane things."

"I'm not going to tell you the same old things," said God. "All

I know is that one day it will all click, and the purpose of everything will be clear." She thought for a minute, and then continued, "I don't control everything the way most people believe. I
just provide the inspiration and the materials for each person to
fashion their own masterpiece. It's then up to that person."

I took a quick look back over my short twenty-year span and
wondered if I'd missed my chance.

"So, what's it like? Heaven, and hell, and how do you decide?"

God's face took on a lovely, proud look. "It's like earth, but
lighter, freer, more golden. Of course, not everybody can fit up
here. Believe it or not, the space is limited. And it's already over-
crowded—the only people we don't want are the truly evil, and
there aren't many of them. I suppose I make the decision somewhere in my subconscious to make them disappear from my
knowledge after they die. I decide everything. I relate it to my
being everybody's mother." God giggled, but then she turned serious again. "What do you think is evil?"

"Hurting someone else—in any way—willfully."

"Good answer. That's the one question I ask everybody. No
fail, just an extra safety net," she explained.

"But what if somebody lies?" I asked.

"You can't lie to me." God grinned. "I'm like Santa Claus. I
know everything."

"So, what's going to happen?" I blurted out. Suddenly I felt
pressed for time, as if I had a million questions and no time to fit
them in.

"Well, heaven is what makes you happy." God stretched out in
her beanbag chair and seemed to think this one through. "It's
what you make of it. Like life. Be reincarnated, be an artist, a
teacher, if you want. Float around on angel wings, or just continue your regular life. You write your own religion, tell yourself
your own commandments. No two people will ever totally
agree. Heaven is really heaven, and it's earth, too . . ."

I stood up, sensing my exit. God opened a door and I caught a glimpse of a beautiful green courtyard. Before I stepped in, I vaguely heard voices . . .

"Jess! Jess, wake up!" my roommate yelled as she shook me. "Wake up!"

"What? What's wrong?" My words, sharp, had more force than a bullet.

"Our class is in fifteen minutes—religion—and we have a test, and you haven't read, and you are going to fail," wailed Sue Ann.

I hoisted myself calmly out of bed with a new sense of serenity and self-assuredness. "It's OK," I said after I had dressed and we were on our way. Sue Ann looked at me strangely, but I knew. *It's OK*, I told myself when I looked at my test paper and saw I didn't know any of the multiple choice answers. I set that aside and took out a sheet of my own notebook paper and began writing—purposefully.

I woke up that morning the same as I did every other, and went to class. But instead of asking myself what it could possibly all be for, I saw my life through a new set of lenses. I now do every little thing with magic and purpose. Every individual person has to make their own way and create their own miracles. My life is my eternal happiness. And I am going to see that I make it my masterpiece.

JESSICA QUILTY

GRANDFATHER'S ANGEL DUST

*A*s I drove home on the familiar two-lane highway one clear autumn night, the sky glistened with the brilliance of the stars. I remember enjoying a breathtaking moment soaking in the beauty and tranquillity of the night, followed by a jolt back into reality with two bright red taillights in front of me.

A car with its left signal light blinking slowed down to turn and then stopped because of oncoming traffic. I immediately slammed on my brakes, but I knew I couldn't stop in time. *Oh my God! I'm going to hit them!* I heard a sickening crunch of bending metal and shattering glass. I bumped my head hard, and my chin hit the steering wheel. An ominous silence settled in.

I stumbled out of my car, dazed by the impact, and saw a woman frantically running from her car, screaming repeatedly, "You killed the children! You killed the children!" My car had gone right through the back of her hatchback, where two little girls had been playing.

This can't be true! I couldn't kill anyone! I thought. My heart pounded violently, and time seemed to stand still. The surroundings were a blur. I heard crying. I heard yelling. I heard sirens in the distance. Then I distinctly remember someone shouting, "The girls are okay! They're shook up, but they seem fine!"

The sight of the other driver hugging the two children brought some momentary comfort as they whisked me into an ambulance. Still, I felt uncertain that they were really OK. The emergency doctor assured me that they were unharmed. I learned the aunt was driving her two nieces to visit their grandparents, who lived on a farm. Miraculously, the woman driver and the two girls were sent home with no noticeable injuries. With a bump on my head and minor bruising, the medical team released me almost immediately.

A police officer walked with me to the door as I left the emergency room feeling shaken but grateful. "I can't believe it," she said. "With the speed of your collision, it's amazing that no one died. You are all very lucky to be alive!"

The next day, I needed to know for sure that the woman and her nieces had no injuries. In my jacket pocket I found a scrap piece of paper with a phone number. I didn't remember who gave it to me. When I dialed the unfamiliar number, the children's grandfather answered. He reassured me that his daughter and grandchildren were unharmed.

"You were protected by invisible hands," he said with certainty. I had to agree. My car went through the hatchback into the area where the children were playing; yet they didn't get a scratch or a bruise. An invisible wall of safety seemed to shield them from my invading car. The wheels of the hatchback were turned in such a way that a sudden force should have pushed the car forward into the other lane. For us, the opposite happened. My car somehow latched on to their car and held it back from the approaching vehicles.

When I hung up the phone, I had an overwhelming sense of the presence of my own beloved grandfather, who had died about a year earlier. But I rationalized that the man I had just talked with had a sensitivity and a wisdom that merely reminded me of grandfather.

That evening, for some unknown reason, I felt compelled to visit my great-aunt, who is my grandfather's sister. I had decided not to tell her about the accident so she wouldn't worry needlessly.

During our conversation she said, "I had a dream about your grandfather."

"When?" I blurted out

"Two nights ago," she answered.

Like a true-to-life experience, she vividly described her dream: "Your grandfather came to visit me. Overcome with joy, I wanted to discuss things together as we'd always done in the past. He told me he couldn't stay because he had to make it out to a farmyard and that he must be there by dark. Then he left."

My great-aunt felt slighted that in this dream Grandfather didn't take the time to talk with her. With tears in my eyes I quietly said, "I think he needed to come and save me and two beautiful girls, who now have their lifetime ahead of them."

HELEN TAUPE

ARE YOU THERE, GOD?

*D*ear God, please help me, went the prayer for the day. And by evening, *Hel-lo? God? Where are you?* Day in and day out, my heart ached as my life spun out of control. My love life with my boyfriend hit the skids, I hated my job, and I hated the classes I'd signed up for. Despair overtook me. Surely this must be what it meant to snap, to go over the edge. Then, in the only clear moment I'd had recently, I thought to myself that it probably wasn't such a good idea to be alone. I called a friend and he told me to come right over.

Crying, I began to tell Andy about everything that had gone awry in my life. In the middle of my tale of woe he smiled and said, "Honey, I know you're going through a rough time, but it'll pass. It'll be all right."

"No, it won't," I protested.

"Yes, it will. Look at me. I got through my hell," he said. Eight years earlier Andy had been in a terrible accident that resulted in paralysis from his waist down. Instead of drawing strength from his courage, I only felt guilty for complaining in front of him. I had to get out of there.

I practically ran to my car. I lit a cigarette and my grief flooded me. Panic followed; my thoughts were in a jumble. Random images seemed to flash in my brain. A scene from the movie *Oh God, You Devil* came to mind. The main character had sold his soul to the devil to become a rock star. He later realized his mistake and asked God to take him back. Feeling forsaken, having received no reply from God, he sat in his house and prayed for a sign. He asked for a rainbow . . . thunder . . . lightning . . . anything . . . and went outside. He got nothing. Feeling dejected and abandoned, he went back in his house and closed the door behind him. At that moment he missed the thunder and lightning—and the rainbow that suddenly appeared.

So, I thought to myself, *why not a rainbow for me?* I closed my eyes and sent up a prayer for a rainbow. When I opened them, I looked up to the sky. Only the moon. I drove home and fell into bed hoping that tomorrow would never come.

The morning came anyway, and I dragged myself to my car to go to work. I looked back at the house to see a brilliant rainbow arching over our house. My heart jumped, and I began to sob the tears that come from being saved from disaster: the tears of knowing that you are loved and protected.

Just then my mom pulled into the driveway. She got out of her car and said, "Melanie, what's the matter?"

"Mom, guess what? God made a rainbow just for me!"

She furrowed her brow and suggested that maybe I should eat some breakfast before I went to work.

Shivers run down my spine even now as I remember friends commenting on how odd it had been to see a rainbow that day—without any rain.

MELANIE ALLEN

SAY A PRAYER

Missing-children posters on milk cartons and billboards always filled me with a compassion for their distressed parents. After becoming a mother, I developed a personal sense of anxiety over such things. Adding a looming facet to my fears was my ex-husband's foreign citizenship.

We had met while I was teaching in Mexico in the late seventies. I came home to the States, he came later, and we were married. After three years it became painfully apparent this was not a good union. His whims and irrational acts kept me bound in daily apprehension over what might be next. Emotionally exhausted, I filed for divorce, only to realize I was pregnant. I proceeded with the pregnancy and the divorce, and became a single mom of a precious boy. Custody had not been determined for the unborn child, but a later court date declared that since the child had never lived with his father, full custody would go to the mother and visitation could be arranged. There were frequent visits, but I always remained present since his dad had no experience with diapers, and I needed to gain more trust. That worked out for a time.

In the year to follow, I met my current husband. We were married when Dan was two and a half. By then, Dan was talking well and could tell me things, so I let him go with his dad for visits a few hours at a time.

When Dan was five, his dad remarried. As I got to know his new wife, I felt all the more comfortable with Dan visiting there.

In the summer of Dan's ninth year, his father planned a drive to Mexico with his wife to visit family. They wanted Dan to join them. I was paralyzed by my old fear of missing children and the thought of my son traveling two thousand miles by car, over the U.S. border, with his noncustodial father. At the same time I saw the value for Dan in meeting his grandmother, aunts, uncles, and cousins in Mexico. What richness he would gain experiencing the sights, sounds, smells, and customs of another land as I had myself some twelve years earlier.

Twelve years! It had been so long. Was anyone who I had called a friend still there? Many of my acquaintances had moved back to the States, and I'd lost touch with those who'd remained. My former in-laws would hardly be my allies if Dan's dad decided Mexico would now be home.

Fears rattled through my brain. The dual citizenship by Mexican law until the age of eighteen . . . social injustice . . . legal injustice . . . bribes . . . the who-knows-who to get what you want. I imagined scenarios suited for the FBI.

Panning back to reality . . . Dan's dad, in the past nine years, had really done nothing to indicate he was capable of abduction. But I still felt uneasy.

And so, with every waking hour, I wrestled with the decision whether or not to let my child venture off on this trip. As those waking hours gnawed away at my sleeping hours, I realized where I should have begun this process, and I prayed. Through tears of sincerity, my heart sought God for wisdom in making the right choice. *Please, give me a sign,* I pleaded. *Please help me see clearly what to do. I'm really stuck.*

The following week we had an exchange student from Israel come stay with us. She was part of an international counselor program arranged through our local YMCA. We enjoyed her stay and stories of her country.

Midweek, host families and international students from the

area all gathered for a picnic. Amidst keeping track of our own four young sons, my husband and I enjoyed chatting with young people from nearly one hundred different countries. Throughout the evening, we were given postcards and trinkets from places on every continent.

As the sun began to set, we gathered our things and were making our way toward the car when I caught the name tag of a young woman from Mexico. I asked where she was from in Mexico.

"Puebla," she answered.

"Oh! I used to teach in Puebla," I said.

"I am a teacher, too," she replied.

"Where do you teach?" I asked.

"At the American School," she told me.

"Oh my! That's where I taught!" I exclaimed. "What grade do you teach?"

"Second."

"So did I. Which room is yours?"

Even the room was the same. As we talked, we calculated that she either took my place or came shortly after I had left. I quickly named a list of teachers I'd known to see who was still there. Many were. By now my family was already at the car. I had her scratch her name and number on a napkin. As she wrote, I marveled that . . . here two thousand miles from that place, amidst students from a world of nations, I found this person in my last glance through the crowd.

When I finally reached the car, heart pounding, I rushed to tell the story to my husband. As I finished and paused, I felt a tranquillity, and then thought . . . *the sign*. I had prayed for a sign. *Was this it, Lord?*

Let him go, were the words I heard. *He will be safe,* my heart beat out. *Those teachers were good to you, they would know how to help,* was the message of comfort I felt.

I sat stunned for a brief moment, tears of awe beginning to brim. I lifted my head toward my husband. As my eyes reached his, they too seemed to say, *Let him go.*

I tried to reach the young teacher in the remaining week the students were in town but was not able to connect with her.

A few weeks later, Dan went on the trip. He called me several times from his grandmother's house. He spent a wonderful week and a half taking in a new culture while forming relationships with people who will always share his heritage.

Thank you, God, for the angels that guarded their trip and the one you sent to tell me it was OK.

TERRI McLEAN

"When I am in fear, please remind me of the chorus of grace that surrounds me."
JULIE LAFOND

MY LEAP OF FAITH

One rainy morning I set off on my daily two-mile walk with my ninety-pound black Lab, Kramer. He's not the brightest or most active dog, but he does possess a high degree of stubbornness. Because of this trait, he wears a no-pull collar leash that attaches to my belt, which keeps him from pulling my arm out of the socket.

On this particular day, we were crossing a church driveway and I was reading the weekly message on the reader board. Suddenly I noticed a car coming from a side street, about to turn directly into the path of a car driving alongside me. Everything shifted to slow motion, except my realization of what was about to happen. Even as the scenario unfolded in my brain, my thoughts raced: *Oh no, they're going to crash—it's wet, they'll skid—they'll hit me!*

In less than the blink of an eye, Kramer and I were scooped up and deposited ten feet away from the driveway. I found myself with my feet in the same stride position they had been in before I "got a lift." I can't explain it—because at forty-six years of age, I could not have performed that leap unassisted. A quick glance at Kramer told me he had landed in a stride position as well.

The cars narrowly missed each other and went on their way. Kramer and I finished our walk, and I had a heightened sense of wonder and awe, grateful for the hands of our guardian angels.

ANN MCCOY

THE GREAT PERRIER WASH

*I*n *the 1980s, an era of greed, I collected people the way* others collected antiques or art. Because my acquisitiveness was so great, I amassed a one-thousand-plus personal mailing list, opened a public relations agency on Fifty-seventh Street in New York City, and digressed from my true life calling as an artist, photographer, and writer.

My typical day consisted of a surplus of superficial telephone calls, telling petty tales of life's happenings, and being a codependent listener to those complaining about their woes. As a woman I had been raised to be that always-available ear. Recounting the past left little time to be in the present.

My life needed reworking! I wanted to surround myself with people I could share truth with. I wanted to reposition some people and edit others out completely. Yet all this realignment seemed too difficult, at best.

One day while sipping Perrier, I sat at my desk and gazed down Broadway. Overwhelmed by the leaning tower of papers in front of me, I distractedly knocked over the large green half-filled bottle of mineral water.

In a split second I watched in horror as the sparkling water engulfed my address book and Rolodex, washing hundreds of names, addresses, and telephone numbers into an indistinguishable inky blur.

I ran for paper towels, but it was too late. Most of the names had been written in water-soluble ink. Only a few inscribed in permanent marker remained.

Panicked, I contemplated how I ever could reconstruct this information. What an arduous, tedious, time-consuming task! As I rested my now aching head in my hands, the proverbial lightbulb turned on.

I began to entertain the idea that perhaps a redo would not be necessary. Maybe this Perrier wash was a divine act—the editorial work on my life I so desperately needed. As I pored through pages and files, I discovered to my amazement that the information concerning the people with whom I shared substantial relationships remained.

This epiphany-like moment started a mindful process in which I learned to choose and value differently those people who entered my life. I discovered a new quality and depth in all of my relationships.

I closed my agency, returned to my artistic bliss, and joyfully reconnected with Spirit following his surprise miraculous cleansing!

JILL LYNNE

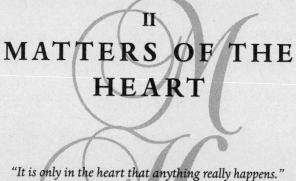

II
MATTERS OF THE
HEART

"It is only in the heart that anything really happens."

ELLEN GLASGOW

MILESTONES

*S*ome birthdays stand out vividly in my mind, like giant signposts marking the milestones of my life.

Time seemed to pass ever more quickly with each passing year, and suddenly my thirtieth loomed ominously on the dark horizon. I slowly came to the realization that I would not be one of those nice little blue-haired ladies who age gracefully—I'd go out kicking and screaming. I good-naturedly tolerated the unavoidable jokes about growing old, and the dreaded date inevitably arrived, then quietly passed. Actually, I was relieved when it was finally behind me and consoled myself with the knowledge that I still felt eighteen inside.

I didn't give much thought to birthdays for the next few years, not until I slid past the thirty-fifth. Then it struck me, and struck me very hard. *Oh God! I'm slipping toward forty—much too fast!* Mornings found me anxiously searching for new lines around my eyes, more wrinkles on my forehead, and counting gray hairs. The nighttime routine grew from a fifteen-minute procedure to an hour-long ritual, with a silent prayer to the goddess of youth thrown in for good measure. Let's just say I had *grown* in more ways than one, and certain body parts no longer pointed in the same direction they once had. Silver threads started sprouting among the gold, and the cost of a trip to the beauty salon more than doubled. All the plucking and shaving, tweezing and squeezing, toning and moaning made no difference. Time, not to mention gravity, was rapidly taking its toll. It didn't seem fair in the least that my husband, Joe, seemed to age like a fine red wine, growing better all the time. I looked nothing like the eighteen-year-old girl that he married, but he continued to reassure me that he loved me more than ever and that he thought I was gorgeous, even though the mirror told me a different story.

Months before my fortieth birthday, I informed friends and family that I vehemently opposed the idea of a surprise party. I couldn't face the public acknowledgment of my middle-ageness. I couldn't bear the inevitable gag gifts of Geritol, Dentu-Cream, and Preparation H. With that out of the way, I had much more worrying time to devote to lamenting my lost youth and fretting over the number forty.

I awoke on *the* day feeling more than a little depressed but determined to put on a happy face. I managed to make it through the long, depressing day and my sweet, thoughtful husband prepared a special dinner. Our two teenagers joined us and were very careful to tread lightly when they recognized the thunderclouds that had gathered overhead. No jokes. No gag gifts. I wondered if they would manage to light all forty candles on my birthday cake before the top melted away and was grateful when surprised with a small cake sprouting just three pink candles—one for yesterday, one for today, and one for tomorrow . . .

The kids went their separate ways after dinner. It was an unseasonably warm prespring evening, and Joe suggested that we take a drive. He headed toward the park and slid the car into a spot near the duck pond. The sun was just sinking behind the large pine trees and he held my hand as we silently watched the day fade away. He leaned over and kissed me lightly on the cheek and told me, as he does every day, that he loves me very much. He turned and lifted a small Styrofoam cooler from behind the front seat and pulled out a chilled bottle of Mumm's along with two crystal goblets. He popped the cork and we laughed when it flew out the open window and landed with a splash in the pond, startling some colorful mallards. Then he filled our glasses, clinked his to mine, and wished me a happy birthday. The bubbles tickled my nose and brought tears to my eyes. We walked around the pond holding hands and sipping champagne. As darkness fell, the ducks quieted and settled into the tall grasses along the bank. When we reached the car, Joe unlocked the trunk, and as it sprang up, the interior light came on. A heavy, sweet fragrance drifted up and filled the still, warm air. The entire trunk was filled with long-stemmed red roses—*forty* of them! The bubbles from the champagne still tickled my nose as I wrapped my arms around him, my face pressed to his shoulder, and felt his arms encircle me, holding me exactly as he did when I was eighteen.

MARGARET J. (MIMI)POPP

GETTING TO NO

*I*t *finally happened—I reached the age where my* No had become rusty from lack of use. Puny. Kind of anemic and whiny. It had been kept under raps during a long period of wanting to be nice all the time, wanting to accommodate. I'm not saying it had completely shriveled up, but it lacked conviction. My No demurred: *"Well, I don't really agree, but it's all relative."* Or, *"Ask so-and-so what they think."*

Usually, unless something terrible has happened to you, you don't lose your No overnight. It is a gradual process of accepting things that compromise you, over and over again, until one day you wake up and realize that your No is missing. What's even worse is that without that clear-cut No, you realize that you don't have a Yes—a wholehearted, from-the-core, you-betcha *Yes!*

A few years ago, I noticed my No attempting a comeback. In little ways, in little moments, my No spilled out in small, inconsequential Noes, like puffs of steam blowing the lid off a pressure cooker. Don't get me wrong; I had spelled out to prospective employers what I would and would not do as part of my job, had engaged in plenty of rousing and noisy arguments with my husband, had fired painting contractors and run them off our property, but all without fully understanding the real process I was going through—recovering my lost No.

It took my two shelties, Rufus and Sassy, to jump-start my No. Sassy is a beauty and a charmer, Rufus looks like a chia pet, or a hedgehog on Rogaine. As a puppy he started fluffing out, and it never stopped.

Rufus is also a social being. When we go for walks, he stops to relate to everyone on the street. If they are busy, he looks at them earnestly until they give in and give him a scratch.

I admit it—Rufus is my favorite. So, when those two German shepherds attacked him on the street that day—they singled out the wrong bear cub.

It took all of us by surprise. One second we were walking in our usual neighborhood—Sassy on her leash, running out ahead, and Rufus walking by my side—when in a flash two colossal German shepherds darted out an open front door, crossed the street with their backs up and their teeth bared, and went for Rufus.

I particularly like those scenes in action movies where the camera is filming in slow motion and everything seems more intense. In those moments, time seems to stand still, and we *see* the things that trigger our impulses. On that day, I *saw* the look in those dogs' eyes. I saw how out of control they were and how small Rufus looked. I knew how hard it would be to stop two of them. But then, just as suddenly as those dogs had lunged out the door, my No lunged out of me, and it was something to behold! Coming out of me like a lion's roar—the Big No. *No! You won't come near me. No! You won't hurt my dog. No! You back off. No! I'll break your neck. Nooooo! And Noooo again!* I lunged at those dogs like a crazy person, bellowing and roaring *No!* A *No!* that rattled and tingled through my spine, that filled me up like a balloon and let loose. A *No!* to blow leaves across the yard and scatter papers—a real butt-kicking, do-*not*-come-any-closer *No!* A *No!* to end all puny Noes and the memory of all puny Noes.

Well. Those poor dogs took off across the street whimpering, their tails low and their heads down. *Bad* dogs. They returned to their master, who appeared dazed. He had merely opened his front door, preparing to take his dogs for their walk, when suddenly, on his own front porch, he found himself thrust into an adrenaline response.

"Put your damn dog on a leash!" he yelled. "If you had your dog on a leash, this wouldn't have happened."

"Yo, bucko," I yelled back, "it wasn't *my* dog who crossed the street. *Your* dogs attacked my dog!"

Silence. Heavy breathing from dogs and people. Nobody moving. My heart pounded in my chest. I put my hand on Rufus's head to calm him. The man with the shepherds looked down and bit his lip.

"OK," he said. "OK. Jeez, I hate it when things like this happen."

Suddenly I felt sorry for the guy. "Look, I'm sorry I took your head off. I really didn't know what your dogs were going to do. Can you understand that?"

"Yeah. I'm sorry, too. They got away from me. They . . . we need to work more together."

"OK. Listen," I said, "do you want to go on ahead of us now?"

"No . . . no. I have some things to do now with them. You go ahead."

It took me a very long time to calm down—almost forty-five minutes, which is the rest of our usual walk. Rufus and Sassy kept looking up at me. They seemed to be glad I was in their pack. Their own alpha mama with the Big No. I know it sounds funny, but I could swear they were proud.

As for me, I'm just glad to have my No back, even if she is a little full of herself at the moment. She is Xena, warrior princess; she is Tina dissing Ike; she is Hepburn to Tracy, Bacall to Bogart. She scans the latest Parks and Recreation brochure for kick boxing classes. She may have overreacted to those German shepherds—or maybe not. But sometimes one magnificent moment of rage that doesn't hurt anybody can really clean out the pipes.

SUSIE TROCCOLO

MARRIAGE IS A CONTRACT, NOT A GUARANTEE

*B*eginnings *are wherever you are, when you're ready to begin.*

Sometimes now it seems that we no longer can dream. But back in ancient times, during World War II, we were good at spinning dreams. And we believed in them, too. Plans we didn't make—because nobody was sure they'd live long enough to have a future. So we just fell in love because that's what we thought people did. The love of your life would come along and all that preposterous stuff—just like the movies.

It was all pretty innocent and we weren't wised up at all, so we just backed into things. Said our terrified prayers, closed our eyes, and jumped. We even thought marriages were made in heaven. And maybe that's where all the trouble starts: in impossible expectations.

I was a gentle only child who'd never been spanked, always been listened to, most often given more than a fair shake. My knockout lover came to me fully combat trained. He was the ninth child in a ten-child immigrant family; it was a wonder they didn't just give him a number instead of a name. But he knew how to scrap for his rights. You can bet your old aspirations on that. Me, I didn't even know we'd just started our own war.

Now, after many years of living by my wits, I can testify that if you expect to have a long, trouble-free relationship, your best bet is to marry a swan.

You have to confront each other, test strengths and weaknesses, lay it all on the table, and—yep—fight like equals. It's yeasty, messy, demanding. But without it, you'll never have much over the long haul, and a ho-hum trip isn't box office stuff.

So, a good permanent relationship requires a number of precise personal skills. Anyone who's doing any thinking and has some mileage is still on fire and hungry for his partner. These people have learned one of life's great tricks: gratitude. They notice that ordinary goodness is, indeed, extraordinary. They see that the luck they have doesn't have to happen.

When I was younger, I went through life like I was killing snakes. Of course I was healthy; of course I was happy; of course people loved me—why not? I was so-o-o-o lovable. My gawd, when I was twenty-five I was so jazzed up I didn't even have to breathe.

But as I slogged along, I noticed that often those who deserve to be loved aren't; that the hardworking can fail, the virtuous go unseen, and the good too often die young. So, notice the good things that come your way and you'll have a better crack at happiness.

By the time two people live together for a long time, they know that nobody can keep his socks up for a lifetime. Each stands before the other—exposed. Acquitted or convicted. Each has a lot to forgive. What's called for is a short memory—and gratitude, lots of it.

At about age forty-five, I decided to take a good look at my partner as though he were a stranger I had just met. How would he look to me if I were some gal in a hunting party and he was fair game? Without memory and grudges and old scores to foul up my judgment, he looked like one damn fine trophy.

And it doesn't just tick down to perfection and then grow dull. Nope. It's not like that. As for me and my combat-scarred partner, we've fought each other as equals.

I walked into the kitchen at 6 A.M. recently and found this note on top of a piece of burnt toast: "Today is our 54th anniversary. How lucky for you to have found me. I'm the best thing that ever happened to you. Love, etc." It was written on a paper napkin.

Now, my partner rarely writes sweet nothings, for such is not his style. Neither does he buy red roses. But next day I was startled to find another message: "This is the first day of our 55th year together. I hope we can be together another 54 years. But I can see that it's really aging me. Love, etc."

Well, I admit that such notes wouldn't do much for a woman who believes in dreams come true. But what they lack in poetic sugar, they make up for in Tabasco hot sauce. And I like the combat zone tone. It reflects a kind of wily, keep-yer-powder-dry spirit, typical of our marathon years together.

So we didn't get there by the book. So we wouldn't look good in a diamonds-are-forever commercial. But shooting from the hip, we got there anyway.

PHYLLIS MILETICH

ROMANCE AND REALITY

When I decided to try my hand at writing, a friend of mine told me that the best thing I could do to prime the pump was to read, read, read. Then she handed me a shopping bag filled with books. A good number of them turned out to be romance novels, and before I knew it, I found myself curled up on the couch on a regular basis, thoroughly engrossed.

I soon realized that reading dozens of romance novels wasn't necessarily going to help my writing, but after reading a couple of steamy passages, hey, who cares?

I'm of the opinion that romance novels are really chewing gum for the brain. I find them formulaic and escapist. Their protagonists are stereotypical. Their heroes are hard boiled, firm jawed, and brooding, their heroines full bosomed and narrow waisted, with long shiny hair and creamy skin that hides the inevitable fire waiting to be lit inside. A fire waiting to be lit by the brooding, hard-bodied hero. Just like my husband, Kirby, and me, I thought with a chuckle, as I settled down for an afternoon read.

Her skin still dewy with sleep, Blaze tossed her mane of silky blond curls and looked deeply into Colt's dark eyes with her own amazingly emerald ones. She lifted her chin proudly, but her full lips quivered, and that touched him. She touched him as no other woman had ever touched him before. Colt, who prided himself on his self control, now lost control, pulling her to him roughly. He felt her soft full breasts heaving against his hard muscles. He lowered his mouth to hers.

Blaze felt her knees go weak as his soft tongue met hers. She had never felt this way before. She felt as if her very core was melting in his white-hot heat. Then she felt his hand warm on her breast . . .

I heard Kirby come in the kitchen door.

"Hey, Lillian! Where are my old boots? I have the septic tank open, but I don't want to get my good boots in it. Man, that tank is *full*. What a stink!"

Not wanting to leave the world of romance, but forced to deal with the world of reality, my mind spasmed.

Kirby stood in the doorway, the sweat glistening through his thinning hair.

Her hair flat on one side from napping, Lillian looked up, her double chin quivering. She looked into Kirby's allergy-red eyes with her amazingly brown ones. As he scratched his soft belly with his gritty hand, he put the cold beer to his lips.

She handed him his boots, and as he grasped them to himself roughly, she felt her knees go weak as overwhelming warmth enveloped her. She felt as if her very core was melting in the white-hot heat of another hot flash . . .

LILLIAN QUASCHNICK

WHAT'S A BODY TO DO?

Recently, my mother plopped a stack of ragged photo albums onto my kitchen table. It was my turn to be in charge of family history, she said. Waxing nostalgic, I spent an evening looking at the faded gray images. Even though the faces weren't always clear, the body shape was. For the first time, I saw myself and my family as we are, and always will be: a family of pears. Barely more than five feet tall, shoulders narrow, hips rounded. With that one swift visit to the past, I realized: *Certain things ain't never gonna be. No matter how much I control and cajole my body, it never will be long and lean.*

I had always believed that if I kept constant vigil over every calorie and fat gram and exercised vigorously, I would someday appear tall and willowy. To that end, I had spent years sipping clear broth, nibbling rice cakes, and making one diet soda last an entire day.

If I was a pear, I was ripe. Right there before my ancestors and the entire world, I—of the size seven wedding dress, iron-maiden foundation garments, and jicama, kiwi, and lettuce leaf dinners—stood up to my lifelong battle of the bulge.

"Baloney!" I said.

My diet fought back with guilt pangs.

I retaliated with hunger pangs.

I went on the attack—Big Mac style. Once I tasted that secret sauce, I knew I had been released from my crudité confines. I was free. Wiping sticky fingers on the seat of my stretch jeans, I thought, *Thank my lucky Mars bar. I am free.*

No longer restricted to the cold aisles of the supermarket root cellar—refrigerated rows of carrots and kumquats, broccoli and cauliflower—I sailed into warm territory. I cruised the bakery with its wonderful world of German chocolate cake and flaky French croissants. From the deli rotisserie, I plucked three French hens. In the store's lunchroom, I scaled the Alps of mashed potatoes bathed in buttery sunshine.

Nearby a portable oven warmed pizza samples that a smiling woman offered again and again. Before, I had stalked celery; now mozzarella clung to me. Another day the sample lady came bearing an electric skillet in which hot sausages sizzled. In a burst of grease-coated cardamom, anise, and red pepper, my life acquired new spice.

At home, I boldly approached the icy stranger my refrigerator had become. Metabolism revved from shopping, I stashed my harvest within. I hummed softly to myself. The refrigerator hummed back.

All was going well until one sleepy morning—old habits die hard—I stepped on the bathroom scale. I would like to say I had somehow lost weight, but you know what the scale revealed.

What the scale did not reveal was that I had gained something besides weight. I had gained peace of mind by making peace with my body. Just as I had looked past body shape, into the hearts and wonderful minds of my mother and grandmother and all my favorite aunts and cousins, now I looked past my own body shape to the real me.

Eventually I settled into a comfortable routine of exercise and healthy eating—neither starving nor larding myself and sailing both the hot and the cold aisles of the market.

My weight, although up, is still within the normal range on my doctor's chart. So my body isn't lean and sculpted, but it's healthy. Perhaps I don't look better in my knit suit, but I feel better, stronger.

I've discovered it is true: a healthy body is a happy body. And from where I'm sitting—on a bit more body—I'm feeling a lot happier. Carrying on the family history. And someday, when I pass the albums on to my daughter, she can take her place among us pears, the sweetest, most succulent of fruits.

CAROL NEWMAN

"Love has nothing to do with what you are expecting to get—only with what you are expecting to give—which is everything."
KATHARINE HEPBURN

SKIMMING THE SEA OF CORTEZ

*O*n a gray and gloomy New Year's Day, after fifteen years of marriage, the man I thought of as overworked but still madly in love with me said, "I'm miserably unhappy with all parts of my life—including you." Rejection stung and shook my faith and perception of my life. If I could misjudge him so completely, then why trust anything else that I'd known to be true?

Chris forced me to confront many core assumptions about myself and our relationship. We both went into survival mode. We fought. We counseled. We separated. The more he disclosed about the breezy new life he'd started to secretly assemble for himself, and the young, carefree biking friends who made no demands on him, the more betrayed and rejected I felt.

Although our differences often seemed irreconcilable and our marriage often irretrievable during that difficult year, we still shared the stubborn desire to live with and raise our two children. That and the slimmest hope of reviving our once-powerful partnership fueled us to forge a new, better-fitting relationship and to rekindle our spark.

In the midst of all that serious trying, we made an interesting discovery. One piece that we both really missed in our lives was travel. We craved the challenge and rush of coping with a completely new environment. We plain old longed for adventure! As Chris and I cautiously started to dream out loud again, a shared future slowly began to look more appealing.

A road trip to Baja sounded intriguing. Having spent part of his youth in Mexico, Chris still speaks convincing Spanish. As a botanist and physiologist he'd longed to visit that narrow strip of land that's home to so many unique plants, animals, and landscapes. Chris's tales of unspoiled beauty and the lure of a sun-blessed family vacation convinced me too.

Striking out for adventure is slightly more complicated with kids in tow. Although we wanted to include them in this expedition, we worried that our very American twelve-year-old daughter and seven-year-old son might not delight in a botanical dream vacation. Baja is no Disneyland. It's beautiful but rugged. Would the lack of familiar foods and comforts be a source of endless complaints, or the beginning of newfound fascinations? Only one way to find out. We went to Baja.

In Baja we were all kids. The sun baked us on deserted beaches, where we snorkeled and swam. We dined on fresh fish, papaya, avocado, *queso fresco,* and corn tortillas. We found an oasis village and cave art, explored local *mercados,* and skimmed across the Sea of Cortez in a small skiff while whales, a cow and a calf, arced together through the waves. Chris and I marveled at how adventurous the kids were. They loved each small town and body of water, befriended every child and stray dog they met.

After some days of relaxing into our bohemian lifestyle, I realized that Chris's midlife crisis was not just about Chris. The life we found ourselves living was the life we'd made together. I have to admit that while his rebellion had been wrenching, it was vital for all of us. His dissatisfaction forced me to examine how I had contributed to our troubles and to look at what type of partner I truly wanted. The kids learned that couples can agree to disagree on some things and work out others without permanent separation.

Near the end of our trip, we found ourselves on a dirt road walking due south one evening, from the Bahía de los Angeles into the desert toward Los Arcos. Protected by wire mesh gaiters in case of startled rattlesnakes, we accompanied a crew of field researchers on their midnight scorpion-collecting hike. Scorpions naturally fluoresce under black light, so their ghostly little forms were easily spotted with portable lamps, then nabbed.

The kids were into nabbing while Chris and I ambled arm in arm beneath a star-spattered sky. Rising above the dusty road ahead was the constellation Scorpio (my astrological sign), shining fierce and bright, illuminating the desert just as our journey to Baja had illuminated our marriage. The magic of being together right then and there was a gift from the universe. We didn't know what was ahead, but we didn't need to. All we needed was to go to the edge of the light we could see and take the next step.

GEORGIA C. HARKER

SIGNS OF LOVE

I'*m one of those people who tends to take everything as a sign.* Is it the last sweater in my size and color? I have to buy it. Do I have a funny feeling about something I'm about to do? Better not go through with it. And gifts? Well, all gifts have some kind of symbolic meaning—don't they?

During my senior year in college, I was fresh in the throes of a new relationship. Valentine's Day was fast approaching, and I searched all over for the perfect gift to signify my heartfelt adoration for my boyfriend. Unfortunately, I'd used all my good ideas on his birthday a week earlier. I searched and searched, but on the big day I was still empty handed except for a sentimental card. He had already presented me with a gold bear pin and a romantic note, and I was starting to panic.

That afternoon, I ran out to go shopping. Well, attempted shopping. I scoured everywhere—the bookstore, the card shops, the mini mall. Nothing. I came back defeated, throwing my jacket and book bag on the floor of my dorm room. I sank into my futon to pout. Almost immediately, there was a knock on my door.

"Surprise!" My boyfriend stood there with a big smile on his face, holding a dozen red roses in one hand and a lush green plant in the other. I was speechless.

"Happy Valentine's Day!" he said.

All I could do was cry and thank him profusely. Whether he knew it or not, he'd provided me with the ultimate romantic gesture: beauty for the moment and something lasting for the future. I felt terribly guilty and wonderfully happy at the same time. I may not have come through for him, but I would come through for us and the little plant. True, I was notorious for killing the poor creatures, but I vowed that this one would survive.

Over the next few months, I did my best to water and love that little plant. After all, it was a symbol of our lasting relationship, our growing love! Unfortunately, it gradually became a bit less lush, and some leaves were clearly dying. But that was normal, right? Just because it was a little less perky than at first, that didn't have to mean anything. I just knew the little guy would make it.

By early May, the school year had ended. I took my little plant with me to my boyfriend's parents' house in upper Michigan, where I planned to stay for a couple of weeks before heading home. It was the first time I'd been there, since we both lived states away from our college homes. I found a shiny silver shelf to set the plant on next to some books. There. It looked pretty and homey. I watered it and more or less forgot about it for the next two weeks. Meanwhile, we had a mellow vacation, ordering pizza, playing Scrabble, watching hockey on TV—mostly indoor stuff since it was still chilly in that part of the country.

The end of my visit was a sad time. I had to return to my home on the West Coast, and my boyfriend and I would have to begin a long-distance romance, our futures uncertain. At least I still had the plant to help me keep the faith. I went to retrieve it from its resting place.

"Aaaarg!" My boyfriend heard my scream from the next room and came bounding in.

"What? What's wrong?"

"Look at my plant!" I wailed. I cradled it mournfully, staring at its crispy brown corpse. There was no green left, and the few leaves left standing looked like overcooked bacon. The dirt had shrunk around it, a clumpy square much smaller than the pot. "What happened?" I moaned.

My boyfriend did his best to contain his amusement and still be sympathetic. "You left it there?" he asked, pointing to where the plant had been.

"Yeah . . ." I sniffled, uncertain about what he was getting at.

"That's the heater. You left it on the heater all this time."

"I killed it!" I wailed again. "I didn't know!" I tightly hugged my boyfriend and the dead plant. "It's an omen!"

"It's not an omen," he laughed, pulling me closer. "It's just a dead plant."

Sadly, I packed up my dead plant to leave. Actually, I cut off a crunchy branch to take with me. Cooked dirt doesn't travel well. I flew back home and placed the branch in my memory box, all the time praying that the relationship wouldn't end up the same way.

It didn't.

Two years later, we got married—despite the trials of a long-distance relationship, despite the stresses of his new life in the military, and despite the little dead plant that had been a symbol of our relationship. These days I'm not so quick to take everything as *a sign*. But perhaps more important, I've given up gardening.

ALAINA SMITH

SEEKING THE FOUNTAIN
OF YOUTH

At a recent photo shoot, the photographer suggested I lean forward and stick my neck out so that the extra skin hanging from below my chin would disappear. That's when I took a real hard, long look at myself in the mirror.

What I wanted most when I made an appointment with the plastic surgeon was privacy and my double chin to go away.

Besides my double chin, though, I didn't see anything else about the aging of my face that was too alarming, considering I'm over half a century old. But my doctor was quick to point out that I had, indeed, aged considerably from that youthful fresh look I must have once had.

When I stood under the bright lights in the doctor's examination room, he offered me a handheld mirror so that I could follow along with him as he pointed out all my flaws. When had that worried crease formed between my brows? And how interesting that I now had excess skin that the doctor could grab hold of between my ears and cheekbones, and eyelids that draped over my eyes.

Never being one to ask very many questions before spontaneously making decisions, I bought his suggestion hook, line, and sinker. I didn't just need to have the skin tightened under my chin, I needed a total face-lift!

I was encouraged to see how satisfied his nurses all seemed. I noticed that every one of them had been "enhanced." One nurse in particular was very excited. She had taken the quest for beauty a step further and informed me it took her only two minutes each morning to look glamorous. To further augment her face-lift, a tattoo artist had tattooed color onto her cheeks, eyeliner around her eyes, and definition in her brows.

My mind began to wander. Thinking of the need for more expediency in this fast-paced world of ours—it kind of makes you want to sleep in your clothes so you don't have to get dressed in the morning, or never make your bed anymore, because you'll want to crawl in again at night anyway, or always leave your bags packed for that next trip—I saw that the options were endless.

The one thing I did that was calculated and well thought out was to schedule my surgery for January 5. Since my husband and I had seen our four grown sons and their wives over the holidays, I figured I wouldn't see any of them for at least three weeks— time enough for me to heal with no one being the wiser!

I heard the first knock on our front door two weeks after my surgery. It was our son David. We stood around the kitchen counter and talked for thirty minutes, and he never noticed a thing. *I'm home free!* I thought.

But then, the next day, Rick rang the doorbell, stopping by for a surprise lunch with Mom. I opened the door and tried to coerce my tight facial muscles into a grin. "Mom," he said, "where'd your smile go?"

That night Pete called saying he needed to be in Portland the next day. Could he stay the night? Frustrated that my plan had been foiled, I thought, *Why not? The gig is definitely up!* He works in high-tech investigations, and within one blink of an eye he asked, "Did you just have a face-lift?"

Our fourth son is in college in another state, but I'm sure the phone was ringing off the hook. So much for privacy . . .

I learned quickly in recovery why plastic surgeons don't explain all the gory details to you ahead of time—no one would go ahead with it! A number of women have asked me whether I'd recommend the procedure to anyone else. At this stage of the game in my healing, it's like asking a woman in labor whether she plans on having more children.

Several months later, I have to admit it's really interesting to look at myself in the mirror. I never know what I'll see! I wouldn't call it an identity crisis exactly, but the nurses were right when they said, "You'll look different every day for the first six months after surgery."

On the plus side, for quite some time I'll have a wrinkle-free, perky look, the eyes of a thirty-year-old, and no reason to ever go under the knife again. My husband says I look cute, and my friends say the face-lift has taken off twenty years. But surprisingly enough, I didn't expect that a part of me would grow to miss the familiar crow's-feet around my eyes and those hard-earned facial creases and sags that disappeared after I discovered the fountain of youth.

KAY ALLENBAUGH

III
SPIRITKEEPERS

"We are not human beings learning to be spiritual; we are spiritual beings learning to be human."

JACQUELYN SMALL

JUST REMEMBER . . .
YOU'RE ONLY TEN!

"I'm fifty this year, and Tannis is forty!" my sister-in-law, Gail, blurted without a hint of shame. I cringed! Having always lied about my age, I was mortified to have it announced so boldly. As luck would have it, my only audience was Betty, whom Gail had just introduced me to. Betty was a grand lady somewhere on the other side of seventy-five (as long as we're on the subject).

My husband, Brian, and I had just spent a glorious week sailing aboard Gail and Bob's boat as we wound through narrow inlets along Canada's Pacific coastline. Glacier-peaked mountains; crisp, clean air; dense, deserted forests: bald eagles swooping down to fish. It was breathtaking.

One day we anchored off Waldron Island in Washington's San Juan Islands to spend the afternoon with Betty at her summer home. Betty was warm and open, and as sharp as a tack. She gave us the grand tour of her charming home, and then guided us on a pathway through the forest. She stopped quite often to point out and identify the names and characteristics of different plants and trees. When we returned to the kitchen she picked up a cookbook and shared a passage with me. She had a passion for and knowledge of life that surpassed those of anyone I had ever met. I was fascinated by her!

As we discussed books and authors, the subject of age came up again. "You know, I have a problem with telling people my age," I admitted. "I never feel my age, so I don't like giving it."

"You have a lot of different ages," she replied. "You have a chronological age, a biological age, a psychological age, an emotional age, a spiritual age . . . so you have to ask people which age they're referring to."

"Wow!" I exclaimed. "I never thought of it that way. In fact, my husband is always referring to me as his ten-year-old."

"Ten?" she chuckled. "I can relate to that."

A kindred spirit, I thought to myself. I ventured on. "I was fearless when I was ten, a bouncing ball of delight. So my mother tells me." She twinkled as she gave me a knowing smile.

Just then her granddaughter Cathy (who must have been chronologically late twenties, but emotionally fifteen that day) came bounding into the room. "Hey, Grandma, we're gonna go down and play on the swing. Do you all want to come?" she asked us.

"You all should go try it," Betty insisted with a hint of mischief.

Fifteen minutes later, Gail, Bob, Brian, and I walked down the driftwood-strewn beach and up a steep hill to where the swing was. I had to tilt my head back to take in the fifteen-foot pedestal, and gulped when I saw a young girl jump off it clutching a rope dangling from a tree much higher up. The swing looked about thirty feet long. She swung out over treetops, then over the beach, arching her back, loving every second of her ride.

Cathy looked down at us from atop the pedestal. "Who wants to go first?"

Brian surprised me by saying, "I'll give it a try." He quickly climbed up the pedestal, grabbed the rope, and took off screaming. We all laughed. But he did it, darn it! My old man! His eyes sparkled and his hair stood on end. He looked electrified.

"Wow! That was some ride!" he bellowed.

Inspired by my husband, I had to do it. I swallowed back a life-long fear of heights and climbed the pedestal. Cathy gave me in-structions and reassurance. I grabbed the rope, wrapped my legs around the large knot, and went to shove off, but my knees started knocking uncontrollably. "I don't think I can do this," I muttered.

Cathy reassured me. "Don't worry, every muscle in your body will automatically cling to the rope for survival. You don't even have to think about it."

I tried again, but my knees buckled under me like Jell-O.

I stood on the pedestal for about fifteen minutes trying to calm my nerves and gain courage as I watched the young girls jump off in front of me, taking their gleeful turns.

I tried once more, but felt nauseous and faint. I just couldn't do it! I handed the rope back to Cathy and thanked her for being so patient with me. Just then, Betty yelled up from the beach, "Have you gone yet, Tannis?"

"No!" I yelled back. "I couldn't get my knees to stop knock-ing." I laughed, trying to sound cavalier.

She yelled back, "Just remember . . . you're only ten!"

Her sweet voice drifted up from the beach carrying a subtle yet powerful energy with it. It grabbed ahold of me, and some-thing inside clicked and shifted! Without hesitation, I grabbed the rope, closed my eyes, and jumped!

A scream erupted from deep within me as a lifetime of fears merged into a giant explosion of sound. I saw treetops whiz by in a blur, and yet every second felt like an eternity. The beach looked a million miles down, and so did my onlookers. The scream kept coming, and I held on for dear life!

As I swung backward, my fear turned into exhilaration, and I started laughing boisterously! Back and forth I swung until I fi-nally came to rest. I jumped down off the rope and bounced around like a dancing ball of delight! I had connected with the part of me that was only ten, and I felt liberated! No wonder I never felt like giving my age! Who wants to be fearful at forty when you can be fearless at ten?

TANNIS BENEDICT

I AM WOMAN

I am woman
Woman am I

Woman of the Morning
momentum on the fly
I am of the moment
catch as catch can
woman of the mockingbird song
watch me in the heartland
Morning Woman, Singing Woman
Woman am I

Woman the Middleman
watchkeeper of the keep
modern mother, wholesale wife
home harborer, gatekeep
spic and span, handyman
watch me do a handstand
Middle woman, Watch woman
Woman am I

Woman of the Moon
wanton and warm
willfulness a whiff, a whirl
within the raffish pearl
romancer, prancing dancer

weave the wondrous dark
Courtesan Woman, Moon Woman
Woman am I

Woman the Moneyman
what it takes in the workplace
worthy of up, up, up
worldly, with no match
I can do it, I can do it
I can do it well
Modern Woman, Money Woman
Woman am I

I am Everyman
that's me as Woman
womanhood, womanland
watch my wingspan
stretching, springing
taking off, wing-a-ding

Woman am I

MARCI MADSEN FULLER

"Faith is . . . not being sure, but betting with your last cent."
MARY JEAN IRION

STEPPIN' OUT ON FAITH

"Sometimes in life you must jump, and the net will come later," says my favorite speaker, Les Brown. But for those of us who cautiously go through this journey with our emergency brakes on, that is easier said than done.

Being a practical person, I always envisioned myself taking a low-risk, secure route vocationally, just as I had done in other areas of my life. I would continue to toil at my job in financial services until retirement—another twenty years. It was in my mind the responsible, safe thing to do, especially after the early setbacks I'd had in my career. Not having clearly defined goals led me to a series of dead-end jobs, low in pay and even lower in gratification, each seemingly taking me further from reaching my true potential. Years earlier, my dreams for college, the scholarship that went with it, and options for a better life had taken a backseat to the many demands of (unexpectedly) being a new mother. Not to mention my credit card debt. I'd convinced myself back then that the employment I found would have to be served out like a life sentence.

I reported to work faithfully each day for fourteen years in a robotic state, just going through the motions. After all, in those days nobody really worked at a job they *enjoyed*. The concept was unfathomable. Even though it felt like I was dying a slow death every day, I stayed. Even though a small voice inside told me that I was not being true to myself, I stayed.

I stayed and I got rewarded. Six promotions, to be exact. However, the longer I stayed, the harder it became to leave. Like a vicious cycle. Little did I know that my last promotion would be the downfall I needed to rise above this rut I had gotten myself into.

My new position, as senior analyst, would entail more money, more responsibility, and a new supervisor, who unfortunately proved to be less than super. Call it a personality clash or ethical difference; we saw eye to eye on nothing. I could never please this woman. The proverbial straw that broke the camel's back occurred one day when she documented some minor errors I made in handling a massive year-end project.

She placed me on a probationary performance-improvement plan and wrote me up. Ninety days to shape up or transfer elsewhere. I was shocked, hurt, and humiliated. Up until that point in my career, I had always gotten along relatively well with authority figures and my performance had always been above par.

The stress from being under the gun each day took a toll. Oftentimes I would come home with terrible migraines. I seemed to always have a cold, I experienced frequent backaches, and frankly, I was horrible to live with.

One day it hit me. As I arrived at work and headed to my desk, I felt like I was walking to my own execution. Tears began to well up in my eyes. It took everything I had not to break down and bawl right there. I couldn't face another day of what had become for me a living hell. I knew then it was time to go.

With no plans of how I would officially support myself (and in the process of a divorce), I announced to my family my decision to quit my job and go back to college.

Five years ago, I said good-bye to the rat race and never looked back. A lot of people perceived my move to be one of great courage. I see it as an act of faith. Once I left matters in God's hands, miracles began to happen.

I received two academic scholarships and attended college debt free. I followed my passion to write. Through a chain of events, an editorial I sent to a women's magazine landed me a future writing assignment. Four assignments later, I became a staff writer. Four years later, I now have a career that allows me not only to make a living but to make a difference.

All because of one faithful day when I let go and let God!

JENNIFER BROWN BANKS

REAL BEAUTY COMES
FROM WITHIN

I first met Mary Jane at a women's interest meeting at someone's home. The first thing that struck me was how different she looked from all the rest of us that evening. Heavy and unshapely, she wore no makeup and had very short, thin hair that lacked any style whatsoever. She wore what appeared to be a man's three-piece suit, and definitely didn't look as though she belonged at a women's group meeting. We all stared at her. I'm ashamed to say that afterwards my friends and I tittered with laughter and made unflattering remarks about Mary Jane's appearance.

I came into contact with Mary Jane again some months later when she joined a professional women's networking group. As president of this group, I needed someone to generate our monthly newsletter, and Mary Jane volunteered. For the next two years, Mary Jane reliably and competently produced our organization's paper.

From this monthly contact, I got to know the real Mary Jane—not the person she looked like, but the personality beneath the external package. Witty, compassionate, and honest, she had a wickedly dry sense of humor and called the shots as she saw them.

As I learned more about her, I discovered a happily married woman with three children. She loved riding her motorcycle in full leathers and volunteered her time to umpire women's softball. She was passionate about umpiring, and it came before everything else. Mary Jane organized her schedule with that as her first priority. As a talented accountant, she gained many of the members of our professional women's networking group as clients. As we all got to know Mary Jane better, we grew to appreciate her eccentricity, discovering that, most of all, she was a loyal supporter and a wonderful friend.

Mary Jane died recently in a tragic scuba diving accident. It happened so suddenly that it's hard to believe she's gone and not coming back. She died as she lived her life—out on the edge of excitement and challenge.

Her dying leaves me saddened in a fundamental way because knowing her taught me some valuable lessons about what's important in life and what's not. Her way of being is a testament that in this fast-paced world of glitz and glamour, there are far more meaningful things than what I look like or what designer label I wear. Unfortunately, the media's view of what I should look like and what's considered beautiful has nothing to do with reality.

I no longer pay attention to anyone's looks; I see their core values. Although Mary Jane has passed on, what she stood for burns brightly in my heart. Mary Jane gave me her precious gift of authenticity and the courage to disregard others' opinions of who I should be or how I should look. She has helped me wipe off the mask of superficiality and not be afraid of being outrageously me!

LAUREN MASER

HIS PLAN FOR ME

Fate was about to change my otherwise uneventful summer. At night I worked as a waitress at a pricey Pennsylvania restaurant that had once been an old barn. The tips were good, and I loved the hours—having time to exercise fiendishly during the day, running six miles by midmorning and swimming for two hours after that. I was training for the women's cross-country team at college and determined to be in the best shape of my life.

One gorgeous Sunday in August, I stepped off the curb with a waitress friend to cross the busy street to the eatery on my way to work. I misjudged the speed of an oncoming car and ran out into the street thinking I could beat it across. My friend, horrified, grabbed my arm and attempted to pull me back. But it was too late. When the car hit me, its hood met my hip and its bumper met my knee, sending my body through the air about seventy-five feet.

That's the last thing I remember. I'm told I bounced, then flew some more before landing in a broken heap on the yellow lines of Route 222. Sirens screamed from several ambulances as firemen and paramedics appeared out of nowhere, along with most of the guests of a nearby inn, who were drawn to the scene by my friend's hysterical cries.

For over an hour I lay unconscious in an intensive care unit. My mother and my older brother raced to the hospital to be near me.

I finally came to, and it was exactly like what I'd seen in the movies: everything was blurry, Mom cried softly as she stood by my side, lots of people peered down at me with instruments and tools, and doctors probed my limbs to see if I had any feeling. My brother, who stared in disbelief, suddenly blurted out, "How many times have I told you not to play in traffic!" And then he proceeded to sob uncontrollably, while I tried to recall what in the world had happened to me. I couldn't figure out where I was or where the throbbing pains all over my body were coming from!

After my family explained to me that I was stuck by a car while crossing the street, it all made perfect sense. I could remember that I saw headlights speed toward me right before the impact. I also recalled hitting the hood. Past that, I had no recollection.

At that moment, I had an out-of-body experience. My body seemed to float about six feet higher than the people in the room. I didn't have any sensation that I was going to die. I lay perfectly still on the hospital stretcher and let myself enjoy the float. As soon as I returned to the stretcher, the pain hit with such intensity that I thought I was going to lose my mind, and I got scared. So scared that I had a panic attack and began to shake uncontrollably.

At the height of my panic, when I began to think that maybe I was going to die, I heard in my left ear a voice whisper, *We're not ready for you yet.* Instantly, every cell in my being knew that she was an angel. Her voice soothed me ever so gently, but her words were as clear as a bell. Peace swept over me like a soft breeze in the sterile and brightly lit hospital room. I knew for certain that all would be well.

An intensive care nurse came to my room that night to advise me that they were waiting for the results of the X rays that were taken when I was unconscious. She informed me matter-of-factly that if the X rays revealed severe damage to my liver, kidneys, or spleen, they would have to operate; the surgery itself would be life threatening, given the potential severity of the trauma. I reassured myself that *they* simply weren't ready for me yet, and an operation wouldn't be necessary. I lay awake that whole night praying that God would indeed spare me. And I replayed over and over in my mind the words spoken by my angel.

When the doctors determined that I would not require surgery, I was moved to the orthopedic wing. There I learned that childbirth, at least in its natural form, was almost certainly out of the question for me. Plus, I never would run again. And my figure, considered by myself and quite a few young men to be in fairly good form, now had a mark of ownership that I was anything but fond of.

But over the next twenty-one years, I would often look down at this rather unattractive, scarred leg of mine and find myself loving it more than my good one. My children, all four of them delivered naturally, call this leg "Mommy's bad leg." This leg serves as a constant reminder to me that I have a purpose in life. God started a good work in me, and he will see it to completion. Not very many twenty-somethings get to live out their life with that complete assurance.

Since the accident, I have always been mindful that God loved me enough to let me go through incredible trauma and pain because He had a plan for my life. He could have very easily taken me when I was twenty if he wanted to, but he didn't. *He wasn't ready for me yet.*

CAROLINA FERNANDEZ

ROOTS AND WINGS

*I*n my early thirties, I was living alone with my golden
retriever, Travis, at Mansfield, the pre–Civil War Kentucky
estate where I rented a former gardener's quarters that had
been transformed into a writer's retreat. It was Groundhog's Day
morning, and I was seated at the old oak table, the same one my
grandmother had played at as a child. A mischievous space
heater that sputtered, sizzled, and threatened my sanity switched
off and on, played dead for minutes, then purred, glowed brilliant orange, and spitted warmth. With fingers nearly frozen, I
persevered—typing the final draft of my play. A sudden gust of
wind from the door, which never quite closed, sent my work air-
borne. I took a sip of already cold coffee and wondered why I
continued to rent the cottage.

I gazed out the window where a tall pine tree, windswept and
burdened by the heavy snow, blocked my view of a formal garden laid out by a nineteenth-century Italian architect. The phone
rang, disturbing the quiet. It was a Los Angeles director wanting
me to come out there for a reading of my play. Thrilled about
the chance to fulfill a lifelong dream to be a playwright, I left the
cottage that night, dog in tow, without even giving it another
thought.

A thousand miles (and every country song in the top forty)
later, I arrived on the outskirts of Los Angeles. Sprawling out
from the San Bernardino Mountains like a giant rat maze, stark,
silent, hot in the pale dawn light, the L.A. freeway loomed before
me. I took the Chino exit and headed for the Chino Valley

Equine Clinic, where a friend was working as a vet. Wire-fence chicken coops, hard, sun-baked dirt yards, and scraggly trees took shape in a dawn already dulled by pollution blown in from the city.

My friend pulled strings for me to sleep on a cracked leather couch beneath the surgery window at the horse clinic. I grew somewhat accustomed to awakening to the sound of metal doors cranking up and the blinding white lights alerting me to a horse being rushed in for surgery.

I learned early on that the director who phoned me would not be making a decision about my play anytime soon, so in the mornings I pressed the only dress I brought and looked for work, pounding the L.A. pavements and waiting in hot rental cars on crowded freeways. Memories of my Kentucky childhood— memories of Shakertown at Pleasant Hill, the garden at Mansfield, and Elkhorn Creek, where I had caught crawdads—came flooding back in moments when I was alone, while sipping coffee in a McDonald's in some unknown town off the L.A. freeway. I walked past movie star names imprinted in concrete, past the HOLLYWOOD sign silhouetted against a bleak hillside, as the traffic roared by. Life in all its curious, wonderful shapes and colors Rollerbladed, bicycled, and danced past me as I wandered sidewalks lined with graffitied concrete walls. I felt like an intruder coming unexpectedly into a film whose beginning I did not and could never know. I kept waiting for something magical to happen, but it somehow never did.

Then one afternoon, I climbed a deserted hillside overlooking the Pacific Ocean and took refuge from a strong wind beneath a California oak whose twisted roots were struggling to hold on to the earth. And suddenly I caught on that what I missed was my roots. Like a tree cut loose from its roots, I was thirsty for the land I knew as a child. I lacked a sense of being connected to the earth, particularly being connected to a patch of soil called home.

In time, a name hurriedly scribbled down as a lead for a place to live turned out to be the name of my future husband. And so I married and moved into a small apartment. Several years later, during lunch at an elegant Japanese restaurant, I looked down at my plate of flowers and fish and realized I couldn't pronounce, let alone eat, a single thing on my plate. I longed for corn bread fried in an iron skillet, spoon bread, and fried chicken and biscuits with sorghum. I missed home.

Not long after that, I came back to Kentucky, bringing my husband with me. On Valentine's Day, we sat on the steps of the historic country church where we were married several years before. This time, however, we were not alone. Our baby daughter, Meredith, pressed a buttercup to her tiny lips, and I lifted her up over a white clapboard fence to watch horses run in grass that was almost blue in the dusk. The air was sweet with the scent of honeysuckle as we gathered violets in knee-high grass that tickled our legs. Sitting together, we breathed in the coming-of-dusk stillness. Now I saw that when I went west in pursuit of something magical, it already existed in my own backyard. Tomorrow I'll bike to Magee's Bakery, where I used to buy birthday cake by the slice after school and a kind clerk behind the counter will treat Meredith to a thumbprint cookie. Later we'll stop by Wheeler's and sit at the soda fountain where locals gather and we'll sip friendship and Cherry Coke.

In time my children will pick blackberries in woods where I once looked for Indian artifacts along Elkhorn Creek. And roots will cut deep—deep into earth nurtured by other gardeners. In the spring I'll take my small daughter back to the cottage at Mansfield. Spring, I think, is the cottage's best season. It is the time when the cottage comes into its own, when daffodils keep company with wild violets in a setting so breathtakingly beautiful that there is no longer a separateness between myself and the land. We'll sit on the porch and watch a fingernail moon rise slowly over the old orchard—an orchard abandoned to the wild, overgrown with blackberry bramble and asparagus shoots.

My daughter slipped her tiny hand into mine and we walked through lawns thick with honey clover. I felt a lightness, as if I was wearing wings. I knew then that I had come home, perhaps to a home I would never have seen had I not picked up the phone and spread my wings several years before. Had I changed, or is it the gift of time to see what has been right before our eyes and in our hearts all along?

MARGARET C. PRICE

CHERYL'S LEGACY

*I*first met Cheryl doing the hospital hall shuffle. Her room was next to mine, and as we began our morning walk, we talked. We quickly discovered we'd both just had a mastectomy from the same surgeon. I remember we laughed nervously like we were sharing some lighthearted social coincidence.

Then the rapid-fire exchange began:

"When did you first suspect?"

"How did you actually find out?"

"How are your kids taking it? What are you telling them?"

"What about your husband?"

"How much has the doctor told you?"

We had just met, but we were now forever bonded through the terror of our experience. We shared the fears we were unable to speak to our loved ones, questions we were too scared to ask our doctors—and the ones we had been unable to even play out in our own heads.

We spent hours exploring our new lives and how we got there. We were both angry and stunned that each of us had received a very late diagnosis of breast cancer, and the question that made us crazy was why our doctors had known so little about this epidemic disease. We were also angry at ourselves for not listening to our bodies, and hiding behind reassuring words from our doctors—words our guts and hearts told us were not true.

Cheryl was only thirty-four years old when she first felt a

lump while in the shower. Terrified, she immediately made an appointment to see her doctor, who reassured her that she was "too young to have breast cancer." She had "nothing to worry about," according to him.

I, too, had found my own lump and was told for two years I had a harmless fibrocystic cyst and not to worry. I felt the tumor growing every day. It grew to be the size of a medium apple inside my small breast. Like Cheryl, I continued to close my mind and blandly listened to my doctor's advice while my body screamed warning signals at me.

By the time we were discharged from the hospital, Cheryl and I had led ourselves through our fears of the upcoming chemotherapy and radiation, talked to our children, and wondered about our sex lives minus a breast (and soon, no hair). We even spoke of dying.

The triumphant result of our time together is that we turned our anger about late detection into action. We decided to publish a pamphlet! We were going to inform every woman we could reach about questions they must ask their doctor. We were going to empower women to take steps so that what happened to us would not happen to them. We had become advocates. We had become activists. Two quiet working moms and wives had vowed to each other to never stop telling their stories.

Cheryl and I went home and began our long outpatient treatments. We spoke weekly and continued to develop *Doctor, I Need to Know,* a pamphlet filled with facts about breast cancer, questions that women must have answered by their health care providers, and a list of resources. I began distributing the pamphlet and speaking to any group willing to have me about the myths and realities of breast cancer.

The work on the project soon became just mine. Cheryl was fighting a new battle. Her cancer had returned and she was buying days of life. Her fight became woven into mine. Cheryl died just twenty months after her cancer was diagnosed, permanently sealing my determination to continue speaking on her behalf.

The last time we spoke, her words were just a whisper. "Lolly, don't ever stop telling our story." Rest assured, I never will.

LOLLY CHAMPION

"My friends are my estate."
EMILY DICKINSON

JOURNEY OF A BRAVE HEART

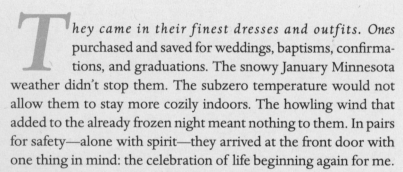

*T**hey came in their finest dresses and outfits. Ones*** purchased and saved for weddings, baptisms, confirmations, and graduations. The snowy January Minnesota weather didn't stop them. The subzero temperature would not allow them to stay more cozily indoors. The howling wind that added to the already frozen night meant nothing to them. In pairs for safety—alone with spirit—they arrived at the front door with one thing in mind: the celebration of life beginning again for me.

It had been a year of bitter divorce hearings and meetings after twenty-two years of marriage to the hometown man that I had chosen in another life. Years of sadness were now compounded with hateful accusations and pointed fingers. Hurts so deep that paper can't hold their truths and hearts can barely survive them. Daughters choosing to support and not understanding the pain of how that support would affect lives forever. Counselors, lawyers, neighbors, friends, enemies all taking an active part in something that was really between him and me. Through it all, I remained hopeful for the time when saner minds and hearts with love would take over the proceedings and bring peace to all involved—our children, me, and even him.

But now, the news of freedom from some of the pain was a

signed decree in my hand. And so a promise fulfilled, that when all was said and done in this segment, I would celebrate with those that lifted me up, that nurtured my heart and soul, that fed my spirit until I was ready to begin again. Invitations were sent to the nineteen women who had understood and undertaken the task of saving me when it was beyond my own power. With their prayers and calls of encouragement, the year passed, and I found myself a survivor at the end. And now as a thank you to all of them, I had my freedom party. The invitation was simple. A 7:35 P.M. celebration with "Brave Heart" as the theme. White Russians and light "hors-divorce" would be served. Each guest was to bring a quote or a song to share with the group that was fitting for the evening.

The group was so eclectic that even I had doubts that it would work. Most of them had heard of the others, but only two had actually met everyone in the room. Artists, teachers, nurses, businesswomen, mothers, daughters, kindergarten pals, college roommates, healers, helpers, golfers, lawyers, family, friends, nurturing souls, they all gathered and shared surprised looks when placing faces with stories heard for so many years. The friendships ranged from forty-five to one and a half years. The common thread that connected us all was their love and support of who I am.

Conversations echoed off the walls and flowed through each room that held yet another friend—another supporter. My smile could not be contained, the hugs were never ending, and the laughter that rang out from each quiet conversation turned into a total group sharing.

And then, the moment I had envisioned since the party first became a thought in the back of my mind: the sharing. We all gathered in the family room—the friend room—tucked shoulder to shoulder, in a semicircle facing the gentle flames of the fireplace. Mom went first with Proverbs 22, next a picture from the 1920s of a woman in a long fitted dress with a wide-brimmed hat at the rail of a boat—definitely on a journey. Carefully cut out and sized to fit was my face on that body, and a CD playing in the background "Free at Last." From Bette Midler songs to quotes from Gloria Steinem, Eleanor Roosevelt, the *Ramayana*, Robert Louis Stevenson, Anne Sullivan, Jean Kerr . . . a book of poetry by Jewel . . . cards with messages placed on paper and engraved in my heart . . . the suitable-for-framing quote from my lawyer that spoke of leaps and landings but was personalized in her own writing, saying, "Gracefully, with courage, humor, and determination, and always, above all, putting your girls' best interests before your own" . . . stories . . . laughter . . . tears . . . and a final song from the musical *Rent*, documenting how to "measure a year."

With glasses raised and clinked after each sharing, we became one in that room. The wood fire sparking us on with each new story, each new revelation, each friendship. The opportunity for me to thank my friends one by one by acknowledging their impact in my life and sharing that with the others. Everyone listening. My friends taking home their own gifts of hearing the stories and sharing in the celebration.

And so the evening flowed over into the quietest hours of morning. More stories, more laughter, more hugs, dances in the kitchen, songs on the piano, and finally sad farewells as time and weather proved stronger than the energy left in each of my remaining friends. One by one they left, some following the car lights of the one in front of them for safety. Heading across the same roads traveled hours before, but now taking home with them the power of friendship and the belief that together we can bring about beginnings that will be blessed by God above and friends around us.

ELIZABETH KRENIK

IV
THE POWER WITHIN

"The externals are simply so many props; everything we need is in us."

Etty Hillesum

"You can't test courage cautiously."
ANNIE DILLARD

HOME AT LAST

When my children went to high school, they both played in the marching band. But my own high school years were punctuated not with the sounds of lively drums and bugles, but with the sound of my father drumming on my brother. With two drunken parents, life on the main floor of our home rang out of control.

I hid upstairs in my room, a temporary sanctuary that offered a shot at a future. I'd finish my homework. And I'd go to college. Somehow, someway, I would go to college.

But when the yelling, threats, and fisticuffs directed at my older brother punctuated the life downstairs, homework sat untouched. I thought again and again, *How can I help?* But I knew that going downstairs would only provoke further violence—this time directed at me.

I assessed my size. At the mercy of a man, my father, larger and stronger, I hadn't a chance. I feared his wrath. I rooted for my brother, now as strong as if not stronger than my dad.

I cried into my schoolbooks. I would give anything to see it end.

Several years later I did manage to go to college. My best education came in the form of psychology books. Some people decry self-help books, but not I. Slowly and surely I sorted my way through levels of cause and effect, beliefs based on fear, and ways to build again the places that had been crushed.

The process was not simple or fast. These constituted bumpy years for my family and for myself. But self-esteem slowly grew in me. As did my spirit. Often my new health didn't sit well with them. So I just kept quiet and continued.

My new life with my own family and home thrived. Most everything worked there, but walking into my parents' home usually felt like walking into a war zone and drawing shrapnel. I felt continually unprepared.

The years moved on, though, and with prayer and self-esteem, forgiveness took a stronger hold. Expectations gave way to compassion. I had reclaimed my soul.

I could remember back and hate the action, instead of the person. One summer's day when I was thirteen years old, my father had suddenly taken me over his knee and spanked me—in front of my boyfriend. My mother watched silently at a distance, without protest. I felt her compassion, but I longed for her defense. I also felt my own total humiliation; but in my home over the years, we were never allowed to talk about it. Very few of us ever even tried. Some kind of tense, unwritten law prevailed.

Now here I was in midlife. Long ago my parents stopped drinking, but behavior patterns persisted, somewhat softened by age. My dad and I finally had gotten a bit closer, but I knew I still hid my feelings. He knew it, too, and wasn't about to change the game.

One weekend I watched a Beach Boys movie. The message: Face your father, face the anger. Resolve it for yourself.

Over dinner the next evening, I harmlessly kidded my dad.

"Don't you do that!" His all-too-quick retort continued, "Don't you know I can still take you over my knee and spank you!" It was a threat, not a question. "And I will!" Within my dad, the bully still lived.

To many people this would be bantering, would even be considered humorous. But different layers of history wove their ugly way within my father's humorless lines.

My life passed before my eyes. I certainly wasn't dying, but something in me wanted to live without fear. *Face your father,* I heard. And all I saw was me in my room, hiding those many years ago. I also had to face myself.

"No. You can't, Dad." The words flowed from my heart like a clear mountain spring finally pushing up to the surface. Then fear crept in. "I have a husband now. And he won't let you."

Talk about hiding behind someone's skirts—even if that someone was my nice husband!

Without skipping a beat, my dad pounced upon the moment. "Oh, then *he'll* spank you." He seemed pleased. Checkmate.

Then I realized we were beyond forgiveness. It was time for compassion for myself. For truth spoken to confront the darkness. Years in formation, a beautiful strength and surety poured into all my being.

Confidently, without anger, I said the words. I clarified. "No, Dad, my husband won't spank me either. No one gets to spank me. *I won't let them.*"

I said it directly but matter-of-factly, like, "No thanks. Don't pass the peas." Only, everyone understood its gravity.

Again, my mother sat by. But this time I needed no defense. I didn't need her self-esteem. I had mine.

I had finally stopped giving everything to find the peace. The peace resided within me.

After my firm reply to my dad, nothing happened. Nothing crashed to the floor. The moment hesitated half a step, then moved on to other things.

But no matter what might have happened, I wasn't dependent upon their reactions.

I smiled, realizing I was home. Not at my parents' home. Not hidden away in a bedroom of fear.

But in my own home. I had built a firm foundation. I had filled it with love—not only for others but for myself.

Now I opened the windows and let the fresh air of freedom in. I loved the home I'd built.

SHEILA STEPHENS

ZOË

My *family works hard to make sure I live a* bearded collie life . . . gutsy, refined, full of joy. Mom named me Zoë because it means full of life and joy. The Big Book says there is a time for every purpose, so there must be a good reason why I can't do what other beardies do. No show ring for me, no best of breed: mine is a family life. Lately I see sadness in Mom's eyes when she thinks I'm not looking.

Zoë was diagnosed at four months with a heart ailment common in female collies. As the vet outlined a future of quiet rest and surgery, I wondered how this could happen.

At six months the vet tried twice to close Zoë's open heart valve and failed. He didn't expect her to make it, but Zoë had a single-minded will to live and the indomitable spirit of a champion. Post surgery, we sat on the cold clinic floor stroking Zoë's face. Despite the lingering effects of the anesthetic, Zoë pulled herself up and wagged a soft welcome.

During routine checkups, the staff marveled at Zoë's sunny disposition and increasing strength. She gave no outward sign of a failing heart. We were told that, stretching it, she might live to her sixth birthday, but we should be prepared to let her go early. Each heartbeat could be her last.

At six years old, Zoë's heart is enlarged and her activity level is somewhat diminished, but we work hard to support her and make each day special for us all, while Zoë continues to defy the odds. Perhaps it's pure instinct, that beardie spirit born of the rough Scottish highlands, but most definitely it's the power of love that keeps us all going. Our family has accepted each day with Zoë as a gift, breathing each moment as deeply as we can. We've learned more about love from Zoë than from most people we know.

At the end of every day, Mom softly whispers she'll always love me, her Zoë. She smiles and wishes she could keep me in a special place so I wouldn't grow older. I still like to get the kinks out chasing my kitty to the front of the house. Mom takes me to romp free through miles of forests and meadows that wrap the city. The highest outcropping is my Happy Place. From that point, I see the whole world and all of you.

This morning Mom announced, "It's Celebrate Zoë Day!" I knew the day was special because after she freshened my beardie topknot, she covered the elastic with my favorite hair clip—the one with the teeny tiny party balloons. I got my own box of tissue to shred, then Mom brought out the biggest purple helium balloon ever and looped it around my collar. At the park, I ran with all the other dogs, bounced along the wooded trail, and barked to let everyone know about Zoë Day. At my Happy Place, Mom untied my purple balloon and we watched it float until it was only a speck. I barked to the sky, "Hey God, look! It's me, Zoë. Today I'm seven."

CAROL ANNE RUEL

LAUGHTER HEALS

*I*n 1987, while sitting on my sofa, I put my hand to my neck and noticed two lumps that were not supposed to be there. I was diagnosed with cancer, Hodgkin's disease. And I knew if I resisted the illness or became passive, I'd get worse. That dreaded word *cancer* taught me to flow with the river instead of frantically paddling upstream.

It's easy to laugh when life is going well, but not so easy when life is difficult. Laughter and my friends got me through. Laughter helps you cope better with change, laughter alleviates stress and relaxes your body, and laughter is going to enhance your resistance to disease.

I believe laughter and tears go side by side. We cry till we laugh and we laugh till we cry. If you're waiting for a reason to laugh in your life, it won't happen automatically. You're going to have to make it happen. So I dug down deep into that lost part of me which knows how to really laugh. Every morning I would wake up, take all my clothes off, put my hands on my hips, look in the mirror, and go, "Ha-ha, hee-hee, ho-ho," until spontaneous laughter poured out.

A certain level of laughter requires a certain level of embarrassment. If you're not willing to be a little bit self-conscious in your life, you won't be able to experience the laughter that heals. If you always want to look "just right," you don't allow yourself the opportunity to be outrageous.

The first test for my treatment was a bone scan at a nearby hospital. I went with my best friend, Marilyn. I wanted to find out how much the tests were going to cost, so we went into the financial office. (I'm a shopper from way back.) If I had to have a disease, I wanted a cheaper one!

In that office I spoke with a woman who was eight months pregnant. When she told me how much the diagnostic testing would run, I started crying hysterically. The only words that came out of my mouth were, "You know, we have something in common. We both have a growth here that we want removed." She chuckled.

At the end of the day, Marilyn said to me, "I don't believe you. You went through all these excruciating tests today, and the only time you cried hysterically is when you found out how much the tests were going to cost!"

The second test was a CAT scan. To me it's like being slid down a hollow tube—like a hot dog being introduced to its bun. I didn't dare cry. I stopped short because I was afraid my tears might cause a short circuit and electrocute me.

For the final test, a lymphangiogram, I went to Stanford Medical Center, in Stanford, California. For this test, technicians inject dye in the top of your feet to see how far the cancer has spread. Marilyn went with me again. When we're nervous, we eat. She and I have survived many diets—I've lost forty-one pounds, she's gained eighty-two, and so on. She carried a big brown food bag that contained salami, sourdough bread, two boxes of Cracker Jacks, three Ding Dongs, and of course, four Diet Cokes.

I lived in San Francisco at that time. When we walked into Stanford, which is a very conservative hospital, the nurse looked at us suspiciously. She asked, "Are you two women from San Francisco?"

I said, "Yes." (They think you are odd when you are from San Francisco.)

"Well, is that lady your partner?" the nurse wanted to know.

I replied, "Only at mealtime, not in life."

They removed my spleen, and I had to learn how to walk all over again. I have dear friends who have the best intentions. One of them brought me healing rocks to put on my belly in hopes of relieving the pain. The surgeon did not understand this. When he came in to check my incision, the rocks were exposed.

"All right, what are these?" he asked.

"I think they're healing rocks," I answered.

He shook his head and said, "Only in California!"

Cancer was a wake-up call. When I didn't flow with the difficulties in my life, my body experienced a physical breakdown. By working eighty hours a week and remaining in an unhealthy relationship that should have ended a long time ago, I was way out of balance. I simply had not taken the time to do those things that create joy and peace of mind in my life. I believe that on our deathbeds, we're not going to say, "I wish I had worked more." We're more likely going to say, "I wish I would have loved more and laughed more."

My cancer is a thing of the past. Recently, while tossing out old prescription bottles, I found one that read: "Vaginal suppositories. Insert until exhausted."

Laughter truly is the key to my success. The average four-year-old laughs four hundred times a day. As adults we laugh a few times a day. I've heard we need at least fifteen laughs a day. My doctors now agree that the more I laugh, the healthier I get!

MARIANNA NUNES

A FULL-CIRCLE GIFT

"*I am pregnant and I can't keep my baby,*" Susan cried. "I want to give it to you when it's born."

The words came tumbling out of the tall dark-haired haired young woman's mouth as though she had rehearsed them a hundred times.

"What?" Surely I hadn't heard her correctly.

She said it again. "I can't keep this baby! I need somebody to help me. If you'll pay for my maternity clothes and medical bills, the baby can be yours. Do you want my baby?"

I had known Susan as a casual acquaintance for several years. We'd never talked about children. Why had she chosen to come to me? Perhaps someone had told her of my longing for a child. All of my close friends knew that when I was fifteen, I learned it would be impossible for me to ever carry a child in my body.

I cried for weeks back then. All my growing-up years, when anyone asked, "What do you want to be when you grow up?" I would answer, "A mother!"

How could God do this to me? My friends and family tried to comfort me. They taught their children to call me Aunt Clara. As a favorite baby-sitter, I was always busy.

Adopting a child had not yet occurred to my husband and me, though we had been married nearly five years at the time of Susan's afternoon visit. Her question hung in the air, and she waited expectantly while my mind raced.

I tried to push back the excitement, to remain calm—to think clearly. It was no use!

"Do I want your baby? Yes!" I nearly screamed the words. Susan and I threw our arms around each other and cried. I assured her that we would pay her medical bills and help her through this. We clung to each other for a long time, realizing that our lives would never be the same from this moment on.

We shopped together for her maternity clothes later that week. During the remaining months of pregnancy, I took Susan to monthly and then weekly appointments with her family physician. One day she asked if she could call us to take her to the hospital when labor started. "And one more thing," she added. "The doctor told me today that it is against the hospital rules for me to see the baby since I'm giving it up for adoption. Will you bring the baby by my apartment after it's born so I can see it?"

"Of course I will," I promised. I could not imagine the emptiness of carrying a baby for nine months, going through the travail of labor, yet never seeing or touching that child. Still, her request brought fear to my heart. *What if she changed her mind?* We contacted an attorney just to play it safe.

I felt certain Susan's baby would be a girl. Don't ask me how I knew. I just did. In fact, I was so sure of it that I decorated the nursery using mostly the color pink. I designed a bassinet cover with layers of ruffles, all pink, and selected a girl's name.

My husband and I rushed Susan to the hospital when her labor started. We sat in the waiting room through that long night. The hospital staff had all been told that we were the adoptive parents. The next morning, against all rules, they allowed us to peek through the nursery window for the first glimpse of our precious little daughter, Cindy.

A few days later, after dressing her in a ruffle-bottomed newborn sleeper and wrapping her in a yellow satin blanket, I carried her into the living room of Susan and her mother's tiny apartment and laid her in her birth mother's arms. Susan unwrapped the blanket, kissed her on each cheek, looked at her tiny fingers and rosebud mouth, kissed her little nose, and declared quietly, "She's perfect."

Susan laid the baby on the couch on top of her blanket. Slowly she folded each corner over, wrapping the package carefully. My eyes blurred with tears. Still I could see the look of appreciation on Susan's face as she laid the gift of her child into my arms.

"Take good care of her," she said.

"I will," I promised as I walked out the door, got into my car, and drove away with Cindy asleep on the seat beside me. We would not see Susan again for nineteen years.

For the first three months of her life, I never left Cindy with anyone, not even my mother, who had successfully raised five children. In my mind, no one could be trusted with this treasure, my daughter. I slept with her on my chest or with my hand on her to be sure she was breathing normally. To have a child was such an incredible miracle. I forgave God and everyone else who had ever made me feel less than a person because I could not bear a child. From her earliest days, we acquainted Cindy with the word *adoption*. As she grew older, her favorite story was of her own birth and adoption.

I recorded all her firsts and special events in a scrapbook: pictures, birthday parties, awards, haircuts, pony rides, school friends, boyfriends, church and school musicals, swimming and skiing lessons, and family backpacking trips.

Once grown and married, Cindy became ill in the fifth month of her first pregnancy. Her condition worsened with time, and her medical team questioned if mother or child would survive delivery. I prayed desperately. We spent a lot of time together in hospitals. One day I said, "Cindy, I want your permission to search for your birth mother. Perhaps there is some inherent health information that will help you." She agreed but expressed no interest in meeting her.

I located Susan through a mutual friend. She was living just a few blocks from her old apartment. Surprised but glad to hear my voice on the telephone, she was unable to add any medical information to what we already had. "I'm so glad you called," she said. "Please come and visit."

A few days later, carrying Cindy's carefully kept lifetime scrapbook under my arm, I knocked on her door. Seated on her couch just as we had been years before, we looked at the pictures of Cindy and our family. Without looking up, Susan said, "I was never able to have any more children, you know, but I have a happy marriage."

"Perhaps we'll be able to enjoy our grandchildren together," I said.

Almost a year later, with her health crisis behind her, Cindy decided to meet her birth mother. As an added bonus, she brought along her healthy baby daughter.

On that day it struck me that we are mothers and daughters together on this pilgrimage called life, none of us owning the other. We are family together in the eyes of God. The gift of life had come full circle.

CLARA OLSON

SOUL FISHING

My troubled mind cleared as I watched tiny droplets of water fly from the line as it arced gracefully across the surface of the water. The sunlight turned the spray into a myriad of sparkling colors. My fly rod felt, for the moment, like an extension of my arm, moving with a grace and rhythm I have yet to experience outside this watery world. I heard the river gurgle happily over rocks and boulders. *Listen,* I thought. *Just listen and learn.*

It had been a couple of years since I first stood in this river learning fly-fishing. What years they'd been, too! I'd been stalked by a crazed radio listener, gone through a very public divorce, and sunk into the depths of depression. The slogan "You've come a long way, baby" came to mind. Yet fear of going it alone continued to plague my thoughts, robbing me of self-confidence.

For the moment, however, it was shaping up to be a wondrous day. Gazing up and down this wide ribbon of water, I could see most of my family members either wading or casting—taking turns untangling nearly invisible line and replacing flies lost in the thick branches hugging the river's edge. My recent interest in fly-fishing had given my family the fever. Squinting through the sunlight, I watched my father cast into a still pool hidden in the shadows of an undercut bank. The surface all but danced with a hatch of insects, and I spotted the quick flash of silver indicating a trout rising to feed. I felt certain my father would have a rainbow on the line soon.

My thoughts skipped along the river's glittery surface, finally giving in to the seduction of a daydream. The image of little Debb at five years of age marched before my eyes. I remembered the day I proudly dragged that limp fish through the dirt, making sure everybody got a good look at it. Catching my first fish has remained one of my first recollections of feeling invincible.

Recently I learned the truth about my so-called first fish. I'm not sure if my dad felt sorry for me, or just wanted to give me the thrill of victory, but he managed to tie that fish onto my line without me knowing it. It turns out the fish of my labor actually belonged to my father. Perhaps I knew it all along.

I found myself smiling at the memory, wondering how long I would have sat on those rocks fishing with my stick and string if my father hadn't intervened. Perhaps it was that same love that prompted my dad's concern today. Minutes ago, he'd caught and released a nice-sized trout. I'd acknowledged his catch with a wink, grin, and a thumbs-up sign. Yet I could see the concern in his eyes as he walked over to me and asked, "Have you had any luck, honey?" Fortunately, I could read my father better than this river, and I knew he feared I'd be disappointed unless I, too, caught a fish this afternoon. "No worries," I replied, smiling. "I don't have to catch a fish to be happy. I always leave the river with something!"

Heading home that evening, I talked to my father about my love of rivers. I found myself explaining how I want to feel invincible again. "The river's music reminds me of the timeless rhythms of nature," I began. "I hear harmony in the delicate balance between this river, the trees, and insects, as well as the fish who feed here." I caught my breath and continued. "Why, I think rivers hold the secret to mysteries of all kinds. Consider relationships, for example." I glanced away, feeling my cheeks redden from self exposure. "Family members, friends, and lovers need to understand when to hold on and when to let go." He listened intently as I continued. "This world and all in it thrive on trust and growth. Roots and wings. The rhythm of the fly rod, the river, the wind, it's all in sync. All we have to do is listen." I glanced at my father to see if he could buy my spiritual ramblings. "Maybe, Dad," I concluded, "I've just grown up and I'm finally listening to all things better. Even the ancient wisdom of river talk." With tears in his eyes, he grabbed my hand and said simply, "I understand."

Later, lying in the soft darkness of my parents' guest room, I thought about the gift I'd received. I closed my eyes and smiled happily. Clearly I knew I was in control of my own catches and my own happiness. I didn't need my sweet father or any other man to take care of that for me. In my own life I will be patient, not fight the current, and grow more invincible daily. Like the grace and rhythm of fly-fishing, I'll allow the river magic to make me strong.

DEBB JANES

LOVE IS FOR ALWAYS

With each shallow breath my husband took, the life I had come to know and love drew to a close. On the mantel of the fireplace—the fireplace we sat in front of on cozy winter nights as we shared our dreams—I studied the twenty-seven bottles of medicine our hospice nurse so carefully and lovingly monitored so that my husband would be free from pain. No one was capable of easing the pain in my heart. Gary was dying.

I remembered the day the doctors gave him just weeks to live, and now as I looked at him and read my hospice checklist, I knew we had only minutes left together. There was not much we could do in those final moments, for he had slipped into unconsciousness, while I sank deeper and deeper into the dark folds of devastating depression.

Soon, all I would have left of the man I loved more than anything in the world would be memories. Gone would be my source of love, my companionship, my minister, my lover. The thought of a life without him left me hopelessly shattered.

As my husband took his final breath, a friend walked through the front door, which I must have accidentally left unlocked. His entrance interrupted my fleeting thoughts of leaving with my husband. That window of opportunity had closed. The hospice nurse came by and emptied the twenty-seven bottles of medicine into the toilet. She explained it was illegal for anyone else to use the medications and threw me a knowing glance. Wordlessly, we knew there was another reason for her action. We understood each other.

The telephone began to ring continually. Although I hadn't called anyone, people who loved my husband called to say they had felt his presence and knew he was gone. One person even told me the exact time Gary died. The alarm on her clock stuck on ten-forty. But my clock ticked on as I did things on automatic pilot. I was aware only of my pain as I braced myself for the empty tomorrows—the most heartbreaking year of my life.

A new school year began. My beautiful students, now third-graders, stopped by for a hug and to inquire lovingly if my husband was better. I prayed I could hold back my tears until later, as I told them he had died.

I decided against counseling and chose to go within. I wrote long letters to God and was shocked when I received a reply. While sitting in prayerful meditation one morning, I heard God's voice telling me that I was loved and that he had a beautiful plan for me. But I clung to the past and almost welcomed the exquisite pain in my heart that had come to stay.

The year progressed and the days brought me all the stages of grief. I parted with my husband's clothes, took off my wedding ring, and came home from the grocery store with dinner for one. I've never known such loneliness.

The pain that ravaged my soul manifested in my body. Strange accidents happened. I fell and broke a toe. I slipped on something in the cafeteria and injured my knee. Just as I was able to walk again, I fell and injured the other knee in the identical spot. What was I doing to myself, I wondered.

As the year came to an end, I realized I was no closer to releasing my husband than I was the day he died. I could easily live another thirty years, and I wanted them to be happy years. I wanted to dance and sing again. I wanted to be free from the pain that ate away at me. Only I could give myself the gift of happiness, but nothing I did seemed to help.

And then I found the answer when I started to clean out the house. Stuck in a drawer, old with age, my handwriting faded and covered with candle wax, was a crumpled sheet of paper. I read my covenant with God, listing the things I would give to the man I loved if He would grant me a special relationship. I read on.

This I will give to the Man I Love: I will support him in all his endeavors and give him unconditional intimacy, loyalty, faithfulness, and trust. I will be at his side to nurture and touch, to heal his wounds, and to calm his heart. I will give him the warmth of a home, a soft afghan to wrap himself in in front of a cozy fire, and a comfortable chair for dreaming. I will give him serenity and harmony. I will listen when he speaks and read to him his favorite things. I will see to his needs and lean on his strength. I will take his gifts and return them so that they can multiply. I will praise God and give thanks every day for the man in my life—the man I love and who loves me. This I shall do.

A deep, all-enveloping peace came over me as I realized I had fulfilled my covenant. I had given my husband everything on my list. I then made the decision to hold in my heart the sweet love we shared and release the pain. A healing hush settled over me.

At the one-year anniversary of my husband's passing, members of our church gathered at our prayer garden and released twenty-four white doves. A friend played the harp and sang a lovely melody, "Love Is Forever." I looked around me and saw my family and friends. My source of love had been here all along. I watched the twenty-four doves wing gracefully through the air—as they flew free. The beautiful birds circled above us for a time, as though in a final salute—a reminder that we all can be free because love is for always.

JUDITH MCCLURE

"Where there is great love there are always miracles."
WILLA CATHER

SCHOOL OF HARD KNOCKS

With tears streaming down my cheeks, I ignored my sister's order. "Get out of here, Courtney!" Penny angrily yelled at me. Arguing with her about my boyfriend was pointless. It never got us anywhere. The end result was Penny's always insisting I pack up and leave him.

"I'll get your things for you," she said.

"I don't need you butting in!" I shouted.

Penny went to the kitchen, grabbed some garbage bags out from under my sink, stormed back into my bedroom, and began shoving my clothes into them without listening to reason.

My boyfriend, Greg, walked in. "Courtney isn't going anywhere, Penny. Put her stuff back!"

"I'm sorry, you're mistaken!" Penny said. "She's moving in with me. A place where *you* won't ever be welcome!"

I hated my sister at that moment. I had just turned eighteen. How could she try to tell me where to live and whom to date! Sure, Greg and I argue sometimes, but it's because I'm the one who comes home late from work and forgets to call.

Frustrated that my sister could be so hardheaded, Greg screamed at her, "Like hell she's going!" and stormed out.

I sat down on the bed and watched Penny gather my belongings. She left behind the pictures of Greg and me on the nightstand. "I'm old enough to take care of myself!" I said.

Penny grabbed me and pulled me to stand in front of the mirror. My face and arms were covered with bruises. "Then why are you staying with someone who beats you, Courtney?" she asked with an exasperated tone of voice.

I stood my ground. "I love him."

Penny snatched several of the bags she'd filled and headed for the open front door. I went after her, trying to get her to listen to my pleas. Greg was blocking the doorway. At first, I didn't notice that he had something in his hand. My sister must not have either. She walked right toward him, and the knife he was holding went into her ribs.

Neighbors who had been outside in their own yards heard my shocked screams. Witnessing the entire incident, they called for an ambulance and the police. I had never been so worried in all my life. On the way to the hospital, I prayed for two things: for my sister to make it through OK, and for her to understand that Greg didn't mean to hurt her. It was just an accident!

Penny never did see things my way or share my opinion. After she made a full recovery, she wouldn't listen to any of my explanations. I begged her not to, but she pressed charges. She betrayed Greg and me and told the police everything.

Greg was held without bond.

Being apart from my boyfriend tore me into pieces. The trial was torturous for both me and my family. Our ties tattered. Hearing each family member of mine tell stories of how many beatings I sustained at Greg's hands made me angry. I felt I couldn't depend on my own family to stand by me and honor my wishes.

Instead of siding with me, they chose my sister. The jury couldn't help but believe them. They were so convincing. Greg was sentenced to one year in prison.

I waited for him. When the day of his release finally came, I was barely speaking to anyone in my family. Weeks later, when Greg hit me again, it took me by surprise. I ran from the house and somehow made it, bleeding out of my mouth and nose, to a convenience store pay phone. I called my mother. She simply said I should have listened to her before Penny got hurt. I phoned my cousin and he said the same thing, adding, "You made your bed."

I must have tried to reach a dozen people. All of them were sick of me, my problems, and my lies. Crushed and devastated, I wondered who would help me now. Only one number left to dial—my sister's—and I hadn't spoken to her since she testified against Greg.

I put thirty-five cents in the slot but slammed down the receiver, unable to handle the guilt on hearing her voice. I curled myself into a ball on the sidewalk, slowly breaking down, not caring who saw me now.

Before long I felt a tap on my shoulder. A bottle of water was being handed to me. I looked up to see who was kind enough to offer me something to drink. My sister gazed down at me with those loving gray eyes of hers. "Mom called, and she told me you needed help."

It took that moment after I had hit rock bottom to realize how much my sister loved me.

"You need a doctor," she asked, "or just a place to stay?"

Expecting "I told you so" or "I hate you," I smiled, feeling that both her offers sounded perfect.

It's been six years now, and I'm married to a wonderful man who would never dream of hurting me. My sister stood next to me as my matron of honor, witnessing the ceremony. We're closer now than ever before.

Penny is more than just my sister, she's my hero and best friend. I often think back to those years with Greg and thank God for a sister who loved me enough to rescue me from my worst enemy—myself.

COURTNEY S.

V

THINKING YOUNG AGAIN

"I shall die very young . . . maybe seventy, maybe eighty, maybe ninety. But I shall be very young."

JEANNE MOREAU

NICKY'S HEAVEN

As I scraped the last drops of yellow cake batter into the pan, I was nudged aside by my five-year-old son, Nicky, trying to do a chin-up on my kitchen counter.

"Mommy, can I lick the spoon?"

His brown eyes rounded with anticipation as I handed him the spoon. His tongue licked the edges, yellow batter smearing on his cheek. "Mmmm, good. Whose birthday?"

A simple question with a complex answer. My neighbor's death, after a long, painful illness, was a blessing, but I wasn't sure how to explain that to my son.

Mrs. Skelton was loved by many, including Nicky. The cake was for her family.

I lowered on one knee to discuss everything at Nicky's level.

"Nicky, Mrs. Skelton died this morning. I'm making this cake for Mr. Skelton—to make him feel better."

Although Nicky's pink tongue wandered over the spoon, his dark eyes never left my face.

"Mrs. Skelton died?"

"Nicky, Mrs. Skelton is in heaven now."

"With Jesus?"

"Yes, with Jesus." As a young mother, I always pray for the seeds of faith I plant in my son to grow into ideas he can use to find his own answers, but I'm never sure I succeed.

"Where's heaven?" His question popped through smacking lips.

I used the simple answer Sister Augustine gave me as a child. "Heaven's far away—in the sky."

"You said Papaw's in heaven. So how come he's in the ground?"

Nicky's ability to weave questions together often humbled me. I was no theologian. I was Nicky's mother.

When I didn't reply, he repeated his question and added, "Nana took me to some place. A rock's got Papaw's name on it. We put flowers where Papaw is. So heaven's in the ground."

I couldn't argue with his logic, so I reached deeper inside my own faith. "Well, Nicky, that's just the place where Papaw's body is. His spirit, his soul . . . it's in heaven."

"You said angels live in heaven. Does Papaw have wings? That's how he moves around?"

"Well, I guess Papaw could have wings."

"Mommy, when this cake's ready, can I have some?"

I relaxed as he asked a question I knew I could answer. "A small piece, Nicky. Remember, it's for Mr. Skelton." I wiped cake batter from his cheek. "We'll go see him later."

"I can help you carry the cake. To Mr. Skelton's house. I'll tell him: 'Mrs. Skelton's in heaven now. She's got wings, and she can fly,' " Nicky announced, throwing his arms up.

"Now Mrs. Skelton won't need that silver thing to walk. She can fly with her angel's wings. That'll make Mr. Skelton feel better, Mommy. Just like your cake."

As he scampered away, I realized it didn't really matter where heaven was, only that it existed in my son's heart. Nicky's heaven is a place where everyone is happy and free from physical pain. It's a place where Jesus lives. Someday I want to be there, too.

DIANE GONZALES BERTRAND

FINDING YOUR WAY

Imet her only once, when I turned fourteen, and for ten years she remained an abiding presence in my life. Before every momentous task, her words inspired and motivated me to do my best.

As a naive, easygoing, and uncertain teenager I attended an on-camera workshop for people wanting to break into commercials. She stepped to the front of the room with poise and self-confidence. She talked about things I had never even heard of at that time: the importance of a positive attitude, goal setting, action plans, and taking charge of your life. Simple concepts in retrospect; but at that time, I struggled with my adolescence. I was craving direction and longing for a role model to guide me through the tempestuous transition from girl-child to womanhood; it seemed she gave that workshop just for me.

Coming into my life as if by divine appointment, her words reverberated and swelled. I rode the crest of that event for the next ten years, using her book like a bible that lay next to my bed. I turned to her book before every milestone: every test, sports competition, job interview, and intimidating moment I faced. I even followed the advice in the chapter on visualization in anticipation of my first kiss!

As the years passed by I wondered what had become of that marvelous woman who had such an impact on my life. I looked for her name on brochures promoting various seminars, but I never saw it. At twenty-three years of age, I decided to become a motivational speaker and modeled my approach on my mentor's example. I joined a speakers' association, and while thumbing through that directory, I found her name, photo, and telephone number! I couldn't believe it. She looked just as I remembered. Feeling joy and surprise, I grabbed the phone and dialed her number.

"You probably don't remember me," I said rapidly into the answering machine, "but I heard you speak ten years ago, and you changed my life. I used the advice in your book to guide me through every important event so far. Every time I came to a crossroads, I opened your book and it inspired me to move on; it assisted me in making important decisions. I can't tell you the impact you had on me. You changed my life!" I left my name and phone number and wondered whether she'd call back.

She did. She invited me to her home and a friendship grew. In the ensuing years she taught me even more. She gave me advice on my career path, showed me the ropes, and shared her own journey. We are now dear friends; her little girl is my goddaughter and our lives are intertwined.

Not too long ago, I felt nostalgic and began looking through a desk filled with my childhood keepsakes. As I sat on the floor, old memories and things long forgotten came back to me. There, in one of the drawers, I noticed the book she had given to me at that seminar so long ago. My bible. As I flipped through, the book opened to the last page, and I spotted her name, address, and phone number—the same one I'd dialed years later—printed in bold type. All those years wondering about her, believing I would never see her again, and I had her number all along. I could only chuckle in amusement that it had escaped me.

I got up from the floor with a sigh and marveled at the ways of the universe. Of course I hadn't seen her number before; I needed to find my own way. While she lit the fire of my soul when I was fourteen, I needed to learn to fan the flames myself. When I believed in myself enough to act from my heart and walk my talk, my teacher appeared. She'd just been waiting for me to show up.

JENNIFER ESPERANTE GUNTER

> *"What one loves in childhood stays in the heart forever."*
> MARY JO PUTNEY

MAGICAL MOMENTS

My frequent business travel rewarded me with two free airline tickets. Realizing the tickets expired immediately after Labor Day weekend, I started investigating destinations to visit. I was pleased to learn the airline recently started nonstop flights to Orlando, Florida.

I have an eight-year-old son named Ryan. My husband supported my idea of Disney World, so I began planning our trip to Orlando.

It was Friday evening of Labor Day weekend. As we drove by the airport on our way to visit someone special in the hospital, my son asked how airplanes find their way from the runway to the gate. We described taxiways and how they were used by airplanes. I said to Ryan, "Why don't we come over to the airport one day and we can watch the airplanes use the taxiway from the gate area?" He liked that idea.

The next day was Saturday. Early in the morning I announced I was going to exercise. That was not unusual for me. Instead of going to exercise I went to the airport to make a deposit of luggage. When I returned home my husband and I asked Ryan what he wanted to do for the day. We decided to pick fun activities to do over the three-day weekend.

Ryan did not hesitate. He wanted to go to a local theme park with rides, shows, and the like. He said he wanted to go only if we could stay all day and into the evening to watch the fireworks. We agreed. I suggested that since we would be there for two meals, I would make some sandwiches so we did not have to spend a lot on food.

We left the house with sandwiches in tow. The big bag allowed me to carry other items as well. Pulling out of the driveway, I said to my husband and Ryan, "Since it is so early, let's stop by the airport before we head over to the theme park. We could look at the taxiways you asked about last night." Since we live so close to the airport, they thought it was a good idea. When we entered the parking area, knowing Ryan loves rides, I said, "Why don't we park in long-term parking? We can take the shuttle bus to the terminal and make it fun!" Ryan was thrilled! Getting out of the car I mentioned that the sandwiches were made with mayonnaise and it would be best not to leave them in the hot car, so I took the bag into the airport terminal with us.

I quietly instructed my husband to take Ryan and walk down a few gates, then return to meet me at gate 2 within five minutes; and then I announced that I was going to find the restroom. While they walked off, I asked the agent at the gate to be part of the fun. As Ryan and my husband approached, Ryan was paged by the agent at gate 2. Ryan looked at me nervously and asked what he did wrong. I responded that I did not know and suggested he ask the agent. As he came to the counter, two other agents watched as the third agent asked Ryan his full name. A bit nervous, Ryan shared his name. She then handed him a bright yellow envelope and said she was asked to deliver it to him from someone very special. Ryan did not know what to do and he was aware he was being watched. I suggested he open the envelope. Out came a bright yellow paper with a message that read:

Dear Ryan,
Please meet me at 8:30 A.M. tomorrow morning at the front gate
of the Magic Kingdom at Disney World.

From Your Special Friend,
Mickey Mouse

He read it and looked at me confused. He told me we could not get there tomorrow. I said, "You're right, we'll have to go today. Better yet, let's go right now!" The ticket agents were smiling ear to ear. They had enjoyed their role.

As we boarded, Ryan, a very astute eight-year-old, asked, "Mom, are we only bringing sandwiches?" I smiled and explained that our luggage was already on the plane. "Mickey Mouse had called earlier, and I knew what to pack." My husband and I watched as Ryan boarded the plane in disbelief.

Of course, I told the flight attendant who welcomed us on board what had just happened. She proceeded to announce to the entire flight that "we have a special person on board that has an important meeting with Mickey Mouse tomorrow morning." The flight lasted a little over two hours. Numerous times I would watch Ryan take out the letter and read it over and over. The emotions he experienced were so memorable. A few people seated nearby got wind of what was happening and added to the excitement by asking Ryan what he would say to Mickey Mouse when he saw him in the morning. One older man turned to me and said, "The memory you are creating for him will last a lifetime. He is a lucky boy to have you as parents." My husband and I smiled with gratitude. As we approached Orlando the flight attendant again announced Ryan's important meeting with Mickey Mouse and asked Ryan to tell Mickey that their airline brought him to Orlando safely and on time. As people were departing the airplane you could hear some ask, "Who's Ryan?"

We had one full day at Disney World and spent it at the Magic Kingdom from 8:30 A.M. until 11:30 P.M. When we arrived at the gate, I told Ryan that the ticket taker told us Mickey Mouse was busy at the moment and that he would catch up with us later. Ryan was fine with the explanation.

We were on a return flight at noon on Monday and back home by 2 P.M. As I said good night to Ryan at the end of the Labor Day weekend he asked me, "Did Mickey Mouse really send this letter to me?" I put my hand over my heart and said, "If you believe it in your heart, you will know it to be true." He smiled, gave me a big hug and kiss, and said, "Mom, you make the best memories. I will remember this trip forever."

JAYNE GARRETT

"Children embrace the ordinary with enchantment . . ."
VIRGINIA DIXON

THE DANCE

When our oldest child was born, thirteen years ago, her father and I . . . well, OK . . . mostly I made the decision that I would work outside of our home on a part-time basis only, during these child-rearing years. I just felt very strongly that there were phases and happenings in my children's young lives that I simply did not want to miss out on! Recently I experienced just such a moment.

It was a warm late-summer eve—the kind that beckons you to stay outside just a while longer because you know that just around the corner loom crisp autumn nights. My three-year-old son and I started off through the timber. Much to our delight, the leaves were enjoying their final stages of green, the air was cool and refreshing, and the fireflies were putting on a lovely show on this particular evening.

We walked through the woods and found ourselves at the spring—nature's water source that bubbles out of the ground right into an old-fashioned claw-foot bathtub that our neighbors have placed just so to catch the clear water.

It is a perfect spot to cup your hands together, gather the frigid water in them, and lift them to your lips for a cool drink. My son and I call it "drinking like the cowboys do."

We started to venture back home, taking our time and enjoying a wonderful conversation in three-year-old phrases about fireflies, cowboys, trucks, cars, puppies, and, well, you know what I mean if ever you have shared some time chatting with a three-year-old boy!

In midconversation, my son turned to me and said, "Mommy, shall we dance?"

I will never know what inspired him to ask me to be his partner at that particular moment, but I can tell you that never has the ballroom been so grand, or my dancing partner so attentive, or the music so majestic as on that evening when the trees and early stars formed our canopy and the humming crickets and June bugs became our orchestra.

He bowed and I curtsied as we began our minuet. How quickly my son transformed from a cowboy to a ballroom dancer. And how quickly I fell in love with that three-year-old all over again.

When the laundry piles up, and the casserole has run over in the newly cleaned oven, and the dog has just dug up your prize-winning flower bed—let us remember moments like this!

CHRISTI KROMMINGA

THE PAPER-CLIP NECKLACE

"*There comes a time in every young man's life* when he no longer wants to kiss his mother good night," or so I was told. I have four sons and was reluctant to believe this old wives' tale. Then it happened to me.

It started gradually. My then eight-year-old son, Miles, would quickly kiss me before the bus rounded the corner toward our driveway. I didn't notice this as a pattern until the day the bus rounded the corner before Miles had the chance to kiss me goodbye. To my surprise, he refused to come near me and quickly hopped on the bus without so much as a peck on the cheek! I watched the bus pull away. With a hollowness in my stomach, I realized that it was happening to me; my firstborn (and most affectionate) child was growing up and away from me!

At first, Miles's reluctance toward any physical contact with me was only in public. He would no longer hold my hand or hug me in front of others. When I told him that I loved him, he would still say, "I love you, too, Mom," but very quickly and only in a whisper. I tried to ease his awkwardness by telling him that it was OK to kiss my cheek instead of my lips now that he was getting older. This seemed to relieve some of his tension. A young girl from school started to call him on the phone at about this time. He never shared any information about her with me. (His little brother told me her name and grade, however.) I tried to take these new arrangements in stride and not too personally. Besides, I told myself, eventually he will come back around.

Six months passed by. Miles and I were more comfortable

with each other, although he rarely touched me or sat very close to me. (It was at this time that I noticed that he still sat close to his father while watching television and would kiss him good night with no hesitation!) He had just celebrated his ninth birthday, and I started to think he would never show affection toward me again. To my surprise, as I was talking on the phone one afternoon, Miles presented me with a necklace made from colored paper clips.

"Is this for me?" I asked. He nodded and smiled as he laid it down beside me. He bounded away before I could grab him, but my heart felt as though I had been given the hug of a lifetime.

Miles expresses his love for me differently now. We share jokes and play cards, and he wants me there at all of his soccer games. He will never again crawl up on my lap to read a story, or ask me to rock him before he goes to sleep, but Miles still loves me. And when I have doubts, I look at my paper-clip necklace to prove it.

JENNIFER HOWARD

A DAD NAMED JOHNNY

Johnny was my friend and benefactor long before he became my stepdad. I grew up in a village in Ohio and he was the fair-haired, gregarious cop on the block. Almost everyone knew him, as much for his golf game as as a symbol of the law. When my parents divorced, I was actually relieved that it was Johnny, and not some stranger, who put the sparkle back in my mother's eyes.

Even before he married my mother, he was always there for me. When the wind off Lake Erie was cutting cold and the air so burdened with snow you couldn't see your neighbor's house, I would look out the window of the Swedish bakery where I worked after school and see his car waiting to drive me home. He was the ice cream man on hot, steamy days and my patient driving instructor when I turned fifteen and parallel-parked into the trunk of a maple tree.

I never meant to disappoint him, but I was more than a teenage challenge. Johnny would suggest not to date a certain boy because of his speeding record, and I would date him. When he cautioned against night driving to Cedar Point in my friend's old broken-down Dodge (under pretense of going to a sleepover), we girls went to Cedar Point and partied until dawn. And when he warned that putting peroxide on your hair could do strange things, I bought two bottles of the stuff and doused my hair with it. I wanted to be blond. I wasn't. I was not exactly a redhead either—more like the color of spoiled carrot juice. The next day, Johnny drove me to school and never asked why I wore a scarf to cover my hair. Sister Mary Agnes made me take it off and instantly called my mother. I was suspended until my hair was "fixed." The beauty salon bleached it out, but my hair was in such bad shape, I was Blondie for a month. I spent the entire time avoiding Sister's glares.

I married young, and the babies came one after the other, four girls. Grandpa Johnny contributed gallons of ice cream and dollars for piggy banks.

I will never forget one day when the sky turned very dark and still. Tornado warnings were broadcast on the radio. When I called the girls inside from playing in the front yard, I discovered my three-year-old had gone off on her tricycle. I called and searched the neighborhood until I was screaming her name, but there was no sign of her.

The sky became even more ominous. Panicked, I dashed to the phone and called Johnny. He sped to the house in his patrol car. When I saw him, a calm descended over me and I told myself everything would be OK. His experience as a cop searching for small children was in our favor. He asked me to stay on the front porch with the girls in case my little wanderer returned home. Then he began walking up and down the block, knocking on doors, giving a description and asking if anyone had seen my daughter. The neighbors who earlier had helped search were now heading to the safe haven of their basements. It was only midafternoon, but the sky was darker than I had ever seen it, and scary. We were running out of time. I felt hollow and frightened, but I still had prayer inside of me, and I begged God for my three-year-old's safe return.

When I saw Johnny's police car coming down the street, I ran down the steps and rushed to the curb. When he walked from the car, he had his great grin on his face, and cradled in his arms was my little girl. He had found her asleep under a nearby porch. Johnny frowned up at the sky. "We'd better be headin' for the basement."

The tornado came with a vengeance and did damage to many of the houses around us. Not even a shutter was blown from our house, and no one was seriously injured.

On this day—more than any other—I experienced overwhelming gratitude for this gentle, insightful man who taught me faith, loved me as a daughter, passed on his values, and prepared me for life. As he patiently explained to my daughter why little children need to stay in their yard when told to do so, I realized dads and grandfathers are wonderful and necessary, but caring stepfathers are gifts.

JOAN ROELKE

VI
POSITIVELY
INTUITIVE

"When you let go, you grow still and silent. You learn to sit among the cornstalks and wait with God."

Sue Monk Kidd

BODY WISE

*I*t began as a foreboding dream in late March. *In the* dream, I walked into the family dining room. On the table lay brightly colored brochures. I stopped for a better look. The brochures were from an oncologist's office, the one on top titled *Everything You Need to Know About the Use of Chemotherapy*. I shook off the dream as one of those crazy games your mind plays when it's tired. I was fine. I wasn't sick. But I still had a queasy feeling that wouldn't go away.

For the next three months, for reasons I couldn't explain, a dark cloud followed me everywhere. Even though my work as a community relations representative for a children's psychiatric department kept me hopping, I wasn't able to shrug off the mood. After days spent crying in my office for no apparent reason, I heeded my gut instinct and made a doctor's appointment.

During my exam the doctor discussed the advisability of a mammogram. *That's it,* I thought. *Breast cancer.* I'd been very good about having yearly mammograms, but this time the technician ordered an ultrasound, mostly to alleviate my concerns. "The X ray and ultrasound look normal. Nothing to worry about," said my technician. On the way home, I scolded myself for the months of emotional turmoil I'd put myself and everyone close to me through.

Five years and a job change passed without further fear or bad dreams. I poured my energy into raising our two teenagers, marketing my new business, and presenting motivational messages for women. Life was good until the day I felt the lump. It left me stunned. I have to admit I'd been remiss with the breast self-exams. I had reasoned them away. I didn't know what a lump should feel like, and, besides, I'd gone in for a breast exam and mammogram every year for the past five years.

I called a specialist. The mammogram didn't show the tumor, but the ultrasound broke the silence. There was a large mass in my left breast. The news came hard, and like most women who hear the C-word, I went into a cold, musty, lonely, dark hole right there in the oncologist's consulting room. She spoke to me, but I couldn't comprehend anything beyond what she said about my tumor being about five years old. I remembered the dream five years ago, the colored brochures, the uneasiness in my body, the exam and ultrasound that gave me a clean bill of health. I left her office angry, thinking, *What's wrong with everyone? Don't they realize I've received terrible news?* The world went about its business as if nothing had happened. A feeling of aloneness overwhelmed me.

My husband received the news quietly, and after a few moments he looked me in the eye and said, "We're going to get through this together." Truer words were never spoken. He came to every office visit and chemo treatment. He sat in the hospital for hours and days without leaving and through it all never swayed from his conviction that I'd get through the treatment and emerge healthy. The power of the human spirit is awesome; the love between two people can withstand any crisis. My husband's determination and faith empowered the positive in me, and God, through this experience, taught me to fight, not against my cancer but for life.

I've learned to trust implicitly my sixth sense with regard to my body. My body is smarter than my mind and doesn't play games where my health is concerned. After five cancer-free years, I am more aware of my inner signals and pay close attention to messages from the heart. I'm no longer in a hurry— whenever I drive, I soak in the beautiful landscape that each season has to offer. And I now stop the car by the side of the road and take time to marvel whenever I see a rainbow. The colors remind me of the beauty that always shines no matter what crisis life brings.

C. YVONNE BROWN

"Success is a great healer."
GERTRUDE ATHERTON

NEVER TAKE "NO" FOR AN ANSWER

Politics *aren't reserved for government. They play a* big part in business, too. Tired of the games at the company I worked for, I quit on October 5, 1987. After all, good marketing jobs were a dime a dozen on Wall Street. I could find another job, no problem. In fact, I decided to take my time looking. Have some fun. Catch up on my reading.

I didn't count on Black Monday, October 19. The Dow Jones industrial average dropped 508 points and changed Wall Street forever. As one recruiter cautioned, "Let me give it to you straight. You're going to have a hell of a time finding a job." I shot back, "I only need one, and I'd like your help." Securities firms were firing people in droves. Thousands of good, educated people were also unemployed. What were my chances? I didn't have a college degree; and my experience, though impressive, was short-lived. I was scared.

Then I read an ad in the *New York Times* that sounded perfect. A bank looking for a trust officer to sell trust services to high-net-worth individuals wanted someone with a college degree and experience. I had neither, yet I *knew* this job had my name on it. I immediately called the search firm that placed that ad.

"Too late," the receptionist replied curtly. "We already have more applications than we can process."

"But you don't understand," I said emphatically. "This is my job." This overwrought employee didn't budge. I hung up the phone telling myself, *This is my job, and I mean to have it.*

Full of resolve, I threw on my business suit—unworn for weeks—grabbed my résumé, and drove to the city. Surprised to see me, the receptionist said, "I told you on the telephone we aren't taking any more résumés." I quietly explained, "This is my job, and I'd like an interview." She shook her head. "Mr. Bishop is too busy to interview you. We've had hundreds of applications for one position. You're too late."

"I understand," I said with a smile and a nod.

I sat down in one of their lobby chairs. Quietly, I told the receptionist, "I'll wait. Maybe he'll have a minute to talk to me. After all, since I'm the right person, he won't have to go through all those résumés. It could be a real time-saver for him." I laughed. She didn't. *She doesn't know me very well, but she will,* I thought. *This is going to be fun.* All my instincts told me this was my job, and I couldn't take "No" for an answer. I'd wait forever if I had to. Besides, I didn't have anything else to do. One thing unemployed people have is plenty of free time!

I sat and I sat. The receptionist glanced up at me from time to time, and I smiled. And I sat and sat. Finally, unnerved, she said, "You're too late, and Mr. Bishop is too busy. You'd better leave." I responded that I understood, but I still wanted to wait until he had a minute.

The day ended, and I never laid eyes on Mr. Bishop. "I'll be back tomorrow," I told the receptionist. "I'm unemployed, so I have all day. I just want an interview, then if the answer is 'No,' I'll leave. But I won't give up without getting an interview." By this time, she looked wide eyed in response to my audacity.

I showed up at the agency at nine-thirty the next morning. Full of fun and energy, I held fast to the challenge. The receptionist seemed surprised to see me. By midmorning, she let go of her "You're too late" mantra, and we became fast friends. Her name was Patty, and she confided that Mr. Bishop felt like a prisoner in his office. He couldn't even go the men's room because he had to walk by me. Other employees in the office smiled as they walked past me to and from the hallway. I talked with everybody. But no Mr. Bishop.

By lunchtime, Mr. Bishop finally caved. Shaking his head and muttering to himself, he called me into his office. I suggested my tactics were perfect for someone applying for a marketing job. Rejection slips off me like olive oil in a Teflon pan. He laughed out loud and told me he'd never had an interview experience like this before.

After he reviewed my résumé, Mr. Bishop picked up the telephone, called the bank, and sent me right over. My unorthodox approach worked. Within two weeks I had one of the best jobs of my life.

In spite of all my resolve to never take "No" for an answer, I don't know who was more surprised, me or Mr. Bishop!

KAREN SHERIDAN

INTUITIVE HOUSE HUNTING

A *few years ago, I lived in a small rented apartment* next to a tiny river. I'm a real water lover, someone who needs to live next to a body of it. The sight of a lake, ocean, or river makes my soul sing and my creativity soar. The little river next to my apartment was narrow and hidden by brush. I could just hear the water babble over rocks, but couldn't really see the water from my window.

One day, I woke up tired of the whole situation! Tired of my cramped quarters. Tired of throwing money away on rent. And mostly tired of not being able to see water from my window. That day, I vowed to buy and move into a waterfront home that had just the right amount of space.

I gave myself full rein to imagine all the details I desired in my new home. I visualized a dream home, not a mansion, but a home that my mind could accept as a believable goal. I've learned that without belief, dreams don't manifest into tangible reality.

I could picture myself living in a moderate-sized condominium on the shores of a nearby lake. Nothing too fancy, just cute and in good condition. I would own my home and pay less per month than my current rent. Oh yes, one more thing: since I hadn't saved much money, I wanted to buy it with no money down.

Looking back, it's interesting that I never even questioned the validity of my desire. I knew what I wanted, and that was that! My decision process felt no different from asking a waitress to replace a dirty glass with a clean one, or expecting a department store to refund an overcharge.

While I was driving to work on the same morning I'd made up

my mind to find the home of my dreams, a strong hunch prompted me to turn onto a little side street I'd never noticed before. I obeyed the instinct and found myself on a windy road near the lake I loved so much.

My intuition pulled at me like a Seeing Eye dog, and I followed it. Already late for work, I must admit another more rational part of me questioned why I continued down this road. Then my eyes caught sight of a gorgeous Cape Cod–style two-story condominium with bay windows overlooking the lake. The home's most beautiful feature was the large For Sale sign perched on a geranium-clad windowsill.

My hands shook as I copied down the realtor's telephone number, because I knew—I just knew—this home would be mine! I could barely drive to work. I called the number listed on the For Sale sign as soon as I got to my office. Instead of getting a voice mail recording, I heard the sales agent answer the phone and agree to meet me at the condo that afternoon.

Although the condo definitely needed a good cleaning, the inside looked even better than the outside. The price of the condo came in at a fraction of what I'd expected. I explained my financial needs to the sales agent before he informed me that he owned the condominium himself. He agreed to my no-money-down terms. One hour later, I had a signed contract and a key in my hand. That weekend I moved into the home that I only dreamed about a short while ago.

I believe we all have this superb guiding force called intuition. When we really listen, trust, and follow that small, still voice within, our intuition will bring us home.

DOREEN VIRTUE

"People see God every day, they just don't recognize him."
PEARL BAILEY

GOLD MEDAL

A brilliant blue sky framed the snow-covered meadow across the road. My husband, Dennis, and our oldest son, Kris, headed out with the plow to deal with mountains of melting April snow. The sun shone warmly in the Colorado high country, and springtime glistened in its rays. I smiled as I did laundry on the back porch watching eighteen-month-old Todd discover the art of stomping in mud puddles. He squealed with delight at every new splash. His corduroys and vest were already splattered beyond saving. Hard to believe that he was just three months away from becoming a big brother to the new life inside of me.

A moment later, an unmistakable command startled me. The voice said, *Go find him—now.* Without hesitation, I grabbed my snow boots and ran out the door as quickly as a woman six months pregnant could go. I could not see Todd. I could hear him struggling, but I couldn't find him. The sound of his cries bounced off the rocks, which made it impossible to pinpoint. I raced to the top of the meadow hoping to spot him from above. I knew in my bones that it was life or death. *Don't panic, just keep focusing on Todd.* I didn't see him from the top of the hill either. I could only hear his cries becoming faint. In desperation I shouted, "Lord, just take me to him." Without a thought, I cut through the meadow again.

Then I saw it: a hole in the ice where he had fallen through. The top of his head showed above the water. His eyes were wide with terror. As I raced to him, the ground gave way, and I too fell in the frigid water.

I have no memory of what happened in the water, or how I got us out of there. I ran with Todd in my arms to our house, started a tub of warm water, and peeled off his clothes. I gently put him in the water, and without warning, he gasped for breath and his little fists clenched. He was going into shock. I had to get help. The community hospital was at least ten minutes away. Todd's color turned to a terrible blue-gray as we raced down the mountain as fast as I dared drive. On impulse, I detoured a block to a friend who is a nurse. As we approached, I laid on the horn. Beth ran out. I screamed that Todd was in trouble. She jumped in the backseat and immediately took over his care.

We dashed into the emergency room. I focused on the sweet face of my son and whispered those things that mothers say when their child's life hangs in the balance. I willed him to live. I begged him to breathe. Todd's body, suffering from severe hypothermia, began to shut down. He was, indeed, dying. The police located Dennis and Kris, and they rushed to the hospital. After what seemed an eternity, Todd began to respond. Severely chilled from my own plunge through the ice, I felt someone wrap a blanket around me and noticed that I had no shoes.

By now, word of the accident had spread through our small town. Good friends and Todd's grandparents Nana and Popi came to be with us. The doctor said Todd had been so close to death that he did not believe either technology or medical science saved him. He could only attribute his survival to a miracle—no scientific explanation could account for it.

Recently I waved the Stars and Stripes with abandon and my tears fell like rain as I watched my now twenty-one-year-old son,

Todd, compete among the world's elite athletes in the Nordic Combined event at the 1998 Winter Olympics in Japan. While I cheered along with thousands of fans, my son's face—a picture of drive and determination—filled up the stadium's big screen.

That face took me back to Todd at eighteen months, when he also competed against the clock in the race of a lifetime—and won the gold.

JEANNE EVANS LODWICK

SPARKY

A few weeks remained before I returned to the United States after a stay in the United Kingdom, and I wanted to make sure I could take my cat, Sparky, with me. She had adopted me one day when I got home from work. Nobody ever understood where she came from, but from then on she became my best friend.

With all my other matters sorted out and my ticket bought, I took Sparky to have her rabies injection at the veterinary clinic so that we would have no trouble getting her through customs. The certificate of vaccination she needed had been ordered three weeks in advance from the Ministry of Agriculture, Food, and Fisheries. On the day of her shot, all went well and Sparky received a good bill of health. We now had only two days left before departure.

Returning home, I could not find the certificate anywhere. A call to the clinic confirmed it wasn't there, and the assistant assured me I had it in my hand when I left. A call to the taxi company that drove us home revealed nothing either. By now it was too late to order a second document. We simply didn't have three weeks to get another one. Distraught, I knew that without the certificate, I might not be allowed to take my pet into the United States and might have to leave her behind. Looking at her trusting eyes, I felt a bolt of despair rush through me. I had to find the certificate! The next day I called the vet and the taxi company again, but to no avail. Time was now running out.

That night I had a dream and watched myself stand in the

vet's office and look at a glass table (no such table exists). On the table were various magazines, and inside one magazine lay my cat's certificate. I woke up the next morning with the image of my dream still vivid in my mind. But I also remembered the assistant say that I had taken the certificate with me.

With no more than four hours left until my plane took off, I debated whether to call the vet's office again. At that moment, my phone rang and the veterinary assistant said, "I have good news! Your certificate has just been found by a customer waiting in the lobby. It was in between the pages of a magazine."

SHEILA O'CONNOR

DISCOVERING THE
BIG PICTURE

*I*n what now seems like a former life, I worked as an electrical engineer for a major avionics firm. Successful but not satisfied, I felt devoid of any true purpose. I began to pray for direction, and as always, God answered.

While I was working on a small research and development team, rumors began to fly fast and furious that we would soon be disbanded. Airlines were competing for business; fare wars were cutting into their profits; and as a result the avionics industry began to suffer huge losses. Daily murmuring in the lunchroom indicated that we would soon be transferred onto different projects. We felt like pawns in a corporate game in which we would inevitably be the losers.

I wish I could say I rose above the negativity and complaining; but I too harbored a grudge against those managers who, with the single stroke of a pen, could alter my future.

For my own renewal, once a week I began attending a nonwork-related personal growth seminar to learn how to take responsibility for my future. The timing couldn't have been more perfect. I found I could apply the same principles in all areas of my life that I took for granted in engineering: first design a plan, then act on your vision, then reassess the situation to make sure you've created what you want.

So what did I envision? I didn't know until one night

when I stood in front of a classroom filled with people and spontaneously told them what was important to me. The thought came to mind suddenly and easily, despite my hesitation about participating in the exercise. "My vision is that people communicate, cooperate, and work together to create great things," I declared in a voice so loud and powerful that I shocked myself. Standing tall, thinking clearly, and speaking with confidence felt exhilarating. I raised my eyebrows in surprise and handed the microphone to the next person in line.

How interesting to discover I'd already been putting into practice my vision at work! Communication and cooperation had always been important to me. I knew for the first time that my worth went far beyond technical achievements and that even if my engineering designs faded into obscurity, at least I made a difference in the lives of the five people on my team. I felt fulfilled and content for the first time in years. A week later I received my transfer notice.

I moved into a position where I coordinated the efforts of over a hundred engineers and hundreds of other people working together at Honeywell and Boeing to design and program cockpit displays for the new Boeing 777 airplane—a plane not yet built.

In spite of the long hours and company layoffs, my dedication to reach the end goal grew. Like a woman possessed by a will greater than her own, I knew customers depended on a thousand different factors all working in well-orchestrated synchronization. The project seemed impossible, but I didn't care. Boeing had an airplane to build. United had an airplane to fly. And we at Honeywell had a lot to do to support their schedules. We couldn't fail.

In addition to my regular duties, I wrote daily bulletins to keep everyone in tune to the pulse of the program and brought cream-filled chocolate doughnuts to morning meetings as a peace offering for the long hours they worked. I ended up on a team with senior managers who were trying to improve morale. Yet another opportunity for me to show what could be done when people care about one another and keep the lines of communication open.

Eighteen months into the program, I flew to Seattle to attend another round of customer meetings. I arrived early, and one of my Boeing friends took me out onto the tarmac to see the very first 777 airplane. A team of mechanics worked to ready the engines, so we climbed into the cockpit unnoticed.

I sat in the captain's seat and carefully touched the six flat panel displays that represented over a year and a half of my life and years' worth of effort by thousands of people worldwide. I looked out the cockpit window and imagined the plane lifting off the runway while the colorful displays came to life. *We did this,* I thought. For an instant I forgot my exhaustion and had the fleeting sensation that I took part in something so much larger than myself.

Already emotional after seeing the results of our department's labor for the first time, I left the aircraft and stood back for a final glance. What I saw took me by surprise. Painted on the nose of the beautiful airplane were the words WORKING TOGETHER. I asked my friend why, and he told me this had been Boeing's motto for the entire 777 airplane program since its inception. In a dizzy flash of memory, I remembered standing in front of a classroom full of people, stating with conviction, "My vision is that people communicate, cooperate, and work together to create great things."

Working together. The scene in front of me seemed like a dream. More than an airplane, this glistening aircraft represented communication and cooperation on a global scale. My life over the last eighteen months suddenly made sense. I saw the reason for my obsession. I understood my passion for making my piece of the program work. I felt choked up as I held back sudden tears of overwhelming joy. At that moment, a still, quiet voice in the back of my mind whispered, *Dear one, the answers are within. You really do create your own reality.*

ANN ALBERS

THE ICE STORM

I was teaching students between the ages of twelve and seventeen in an alternative education program. I had gotten this job after a five-year hiatus at home, caring for my son.

Unfortunately, during that time, *delinquent* had come to encompass violent, drug-ridden, psychotic, and out-of-control behavior. A far cry from the slow-learning, mildly disruptive students I had taught before my son was born.

I soon found that these students had no intention of fitting in the school population. They made no secret of the fact that they were there only because their probation demanded it. Motivating these young men would be no mean feat.

Before, I could interest my students in work permits and want ads—but these kids were into dealing drugs and stealing. They probably made more in a week than I did in a month. Attempts to interest them in things like bank accounts and budgets were dismissed as outdated and silly.

I first learned about my most powerful motivator when I called the probation officer to inform him that one of his little "court reluctants" was in danger of failing English. I made the call from my classroom and a deathly pall came over the room. At that moment, I could have asked my students to do anything and they would have done it.

In spite of their very tough and supposedly nonchalant attitudes, they did develop a grudging respect for me and would police one another on language or particularly deviant behavior.

I stumbled on another motivator quite by accident. I was driving a 1969 Nova with 150,000 miles on it. There wasn't a day that something didn't go wrong with that heap. The kids were fascinated with the antics I had to go through to get it started and keep it going—sticking a ruler in the carburetor so it wouldn't flood while I was trying to start it, priming the radiator so it wouldn't overheat, or filling up the oil.

Watching me perform all of these tasks just to get home in the afternoon peaked their interest. I banked on that and invited Bob, my mechanic, to class. He brought with him a blender motor and within five minutes, they were hooked.

Bob, himself a high school dropout, peppered his demonstrations with admonitions to the young men to behave themselves and take school more seriously. They seemed to hang on his every word, which gave me an idea: I'd give them lots of repair time with Bob if they'd give me time to prepare them for the general equivalency diploma (GED)—a process that would allow them to complete high school in less than four years.

The success they were experiencing was changing them. Their gruff exteriors were softening. In my classroom, anyway, I caught a glimpse of what they might have been if the streets had not taken over. One particular incident comes to mind.

They had become quite solicitous of my well-being and were particularly concerned one afternoon during an ice storm about whether or not I would even make it to my car. They had decided to escort me. I had one young man in front of me, one behind, and one on either side. As we started gingerly down the slick stairs, we were clinging to one another like leaves on vines. It looked like we were going to make it when suddenly from around the back came the rest of the clan, loaded with enough snowballs to thoroughly bury us. My escorts let go of me in order to retaliate and I went down—taking all four of them with me. As we started sliding down the stairs, the other students came running to help, and we all ended up on the bottom step laughing so hard that we were breathless.

I treasure that simple memory of them all piled up, soaking wet, a tangle of arms and legs, away from the streets, the drugs, the violence, laughing and playing in the snow, just like the kids they should have been in the first place.

MARTHA NICHOLSON

VII
WAKE-UP CALLS

"There is only one teacher—life itself."

CHARLOTTE JOKO BECK

AND THE WINNER IS . . .

The day had started typically enough. I had gone to my job in the one-person office that I occupied on a quiet tree-lined street in a small suburban city. I lived a scant five minutes away and enjoyed the safe comfort zone of unvaried work and familiar surroundings. Let other women flail at the glass ceiling. I was content with a predictable daily routine, uncomplicated paperwork, and an established customer base. The telephone rang as I prepared for my usual solitary lunch.

"Hi, Rod. What's up?" I asked.

Rod, a casual acquaintance who fancied himself a part-time actor and model, currently worked installing special lighting for stage shows and sporting events.

"Listen, sweetie, I'm in a bit of a jam."

Uh-oh, here it comes, I thought. *I'm not going to like this.*

"I've got this deal with a talent agent to provide people for auditions. I get a commission for every actor that shows up whether they're hired or not. I had this gal lined up to audition for a soft drink commercial, but she got a better offer and canceled on me."

I leaned back in my chair and let my mind wander. I was immediately intrigued with an ornate cobweb decorating the light fixture.

"The part calls for a mature businesswoman type. All you have to do is ad-lib about how hectic your day was, take a sip of the soda, and say how refreshing and soothing it is. It's kind of like when they knock on a door and ask a woman about her laundry and she shows them all her whites. Just be natural and act sincere. Will you do it?"

"Hello? What? Do what?"

"Audition for the commercial. I swear it will only take about fifteen minutes. There's nothing to it. Say a few words about your busy day, take a sip of soda, smile, presto changeo-, you're outta there."

Warning bells went off in my head. *Hold on, let's get real here. I'm plump, pushing fifty-five, my hair is dyed "copper penny," and the hem of my skirt is being held up by Scotch tape. Slow down. Danger ahead. Apocalypse.*

"Rod, dear," I said patiently, "I really appreciate the offer, but . . . I don't think, that is, I'm just not the type to . . . how can I put this? . . . I don't even like to see myself on those television monitors in the store. I mean, I'd love to help you out, but . . ." I paused. My mind suddenly went blank.

"OK, I'll do it," I said quickly, my spontaneous streak erupting out of nowhere! "Where and what time?"

An hour later, giddily clutching an address in my hand, I rode the train to San Francisco and studied my reflection in the window. Oblivious to other passengers, I rehearsed my upcoming role.

"Citrus-Ade is a girl's best friend," I mouthed to the window several times in my best Marilyn Monroe imitation. "It is sooo refreshing."

The studio turned out to be a drab two-story building on the south side of the city. Entering, I was immediately given a questionnaire to fill out. The waiting room had several people holding eight-by-ten glossies; a man was reciting lines, another pacing the floor. I returned to the receptionist with my completed application.

"Dear," I said, "this form asks if I belong to the Screen Actors Guild, and I answered 'No.' However, that's just temporary. I intend to join right after this shoot." She looked at me with dead eyes through wide bands of black eyeliner.

"Sit down," she said, pointing vaguely to a line of dingy chairs.

Soon after, the director led me into the filming room and quickly explained the scene to be videotaped.

"You are a busy woman with heavy responsibilities. Think of yourself as a senator or someone like that. You have a lot of meetings. Rub your forehead like you're tired, exhausted, pooped. My assistant, off camera, will hand you a can of Citrus-Ade. Open the can, take a sip, and tell the camera in your own words how refreshing it is. Got it?"

"Got it," I said, fluffing my hair and arranging my lips in a glamorous pout.

The camera started rolling and so did my mouth. Out came a rush of words. Peculiar words, reckless words, incomplete sentences. My lips receded to a thin, cracked line.

A can of soda was thrust into my hand. I held it up to the camera and placed my thumb on the flip tab. I struggled with the can, wrestled it between my knees, and tugged at the tab. As the can popped open, my fingernail broke off, flew across the room, and hit the camera lens. I took a sip of the soda, looked into the camera, and praised the refreshing taste of Citrus-Ade's major competitor!

It was over too soon. I strolled down the street, my feet barely touching the sidewalk. *What did they put in that can? Everything looks so bright.*

That's when I realized what had really happened. I had ventured out from my tiny, safe corner of the world and had taken a chance. I had acted on a dream and transformed myself, if only for a few hours. And now, I never felt so alive, so relevant, so—refreshed!

At the train station, I stopped at a flower stall and picked out a bouquet of flowers. As the vendor handed me the wrapped blossoms, I smiled radiantly and said, "I want to thank all the little people for this award. I wouldn't be here today without your help."

"It was nothin', lady," he said, turning away. "Don't mention it."

I smiled all the way home.

CLAUDIA McCORMICK

*"Talk to God—God has wonderful things to tell you that
you do not know."*
THE REVEREND MARY OMWAKE

THE G-WORD

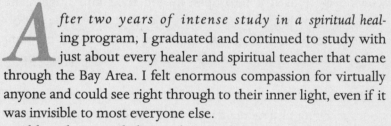

*A*fter two years of intense study in a spiritual healing program, I graduated and continued to study with
just about every healer and spiritual teacher that came
through the Bay Area. I felt enormous compassion for virtually
anyone and could see right through to their inner light, even if it
was invisible to most everyone else.

Although I attended countless workshops and classes explor-
ing our soul, heart, humanity, the universe and how it all works,
I avoided sessions if I knew the speaker would be talking about
God.

Now and then the G-word would suddenly come up, and I
would feel somewhat queasy, oftentimes embarrassed. Discount-
ing the message entirely, I would send my mind off into other
realms. I felt uncomfortable for the presenter, like a teenager
who's ill at ease when out with her parents in public.

Even with all the knowledge I'd gained, as I dug deeper into
my emotional pain from unresolved family experiences the
emptiness inside me grew. I looked for guidance wherever I
could find it. One morning I switched on the television to watch
a regularly aired Sunday service a friend had recommended. The

minister's message provided a lot of wisdom and laughter, but she used that *God* word a lot!

I began getting up every Sunday by 7 A.M. so I wouldn't miss her show. Still feeling embarrassed by the G-word, I would tell friends she had lots to offer, and you can just ignore her talk about God—like something you had to put up with to get the good stuff.

During this time, my introspection deepened as I uncovered more layers of hurt in my life. Moments of insight energized me, followed by a recurring unrest in my soul.

In Santa Cruz, the Sufis put on a session led by a visiting Huichol shaman, Don José Matsuwa. Don José, at 105 years of age, exuded enormous vitality. Speaking in his native language, which was translated into Spanish and then into English, he talked to us of life, adventure, love, the spirit world, the importance of laughter, and many of the rich traditions of the Huichols. I was utterly captivated. A vast new universe opened up to me.

He took us outside to a large arena, where he spent several hours teaching us a sacred dance with lots of accompanying ritual and burning of sage. We formed a circle, and in the center of it we each placed a personal object. I set down an amethyst crystal. On a gorgeous, sunny California day, this tiny man in colorful Huichol native dress led us into other realms, using movement and meditation. I felt the under sea of my life shifting as waves of light rippled across the surface.

Don José explained that in the Huichol religion, everything is sacred, and life is precious and delightful. There is a Grandmother Growth, who provides the nurturing earth energy, and the Deer God, who offers the male aspects of the divine. Their religious tradition includes an arduous annual pilgrimage to collect peyote buttons in the desert, which they bring back to their community to use in holy rituals.

At the end of the day, laughter and joy—that is part of the

Huichol way—bubbled up like a spring from my core, filling me up and washing gently over my emotional pain. I bought one of the handwoven peyote bags to take home with me. On it were symbols of the Deer God (deer antlers) and Grandmother Growth (a symbolic eye). I retrieved my amethyst crystal from the altar we'd created in the circle and headed home.

After the workshop, I continued to watch my favorite Sunday service on television and meditate daily. Now when I asked for guidance, I would see an Image of a deer (a deer head with antlers, actually) that I addressed as "Deer God."

One day, I suddenly realized the image of the deer head had melted away, and I was praying to *"Dear* God." I used the G-word myself! I laughed and laughed, like my 105-year-old friend, holding my sides at the hilarity and wonder of it all.

From then on I knew God is wherever I am, and we have developed an infinitely rich and exciting relationship. I use the G-word often, whenever I feel like it. If I spot a wary look and glazed-over eyes from a participant in the classes I now teach, I wonder if here sits another person about ready to open up to the creative force of the universe. And when I occasionally forget how blessed I am, I wear my amethyst crystal and remember the tiny shaman who was my catalyst for change.

You see, regardless of our path, with the slightest shift in direction, God takes us right where we are and welcomes us home.

MARTHA POWERS

DAVID'S SURPRISE

January 31, 1974, was an incredibly sunny, warm day. It was also the day my perfect life came crashing down around me. My husband, Lee, and I were at home with our seven-year-old son, David, when the horrible news came: our Angie, eleven, had been killed in an accident, along with a teenage girl my two daughters had been visiting.

What anguish . . . what unimaginable devastation.

Immediately, amid the deluge of loss, I pictured David and Angie bike riding together over sandy trails during the six months we'd lived in Shiloh, South Carolina, or playing Old Maid, or embarking upon Password's more serious challenge. While our independent Pam, thirteen, sought privacy, the two younger siblings had bonded closely in this tranquil rural setting. Gentle patience marked Angie's attitude toward her sometimes bumbling little brother. Now what would David do without his doting sister?

What would I do without my little nursemaid? Oh God, how would I get through it? How could I let go?

The following days blurred as family rallied and loving, caring people came and went. Slowly, I noticed that David seemed set apart from the grim drama. His face gave no indication that he felt the enormity of what had happened.

Fear hit me. Would he forget her? From my fog of pain, I honestly didn't know what to say to him, and when I tried—something always stopped me.

Days later, I noticed he'd moved on to more play activity. Annoyance pierced my haze of grief when I noticed him digging on our property's back corner, actually a low-country sand hill with marshy sod in places. His area of interest sloped away and downward, out of sight from the kitchen window. Amid visits from condolence bearers, I was aware of the backyard toil and wondered, vaguely, what make-believe fantasy held him captive.

At first, his solitary activity didn't seem extraordinary, since David now had no steady playmate. It's simply a time-passing, energy-spending diversion, I concluded, and proceeded with life motions and the grieving process.

Day in, day out, David continued to trudge over the hill, digging from sunup till sundown. Perplexed, I asked him, "What's going on?"

"It's a surprise," he informed me matter-of-factly. He'd always been the fun-seeking adventurer of the family. But now, quite frankly, his enthusiasm stirred my anger. After all, he never even mentioned Angie. I certainly didn't expect him to anguish as I did, but it didn't seem right somehow that he ignored her absence.

One day, young friends visited. David merely put them to work. From the window, I gaped at kids scurrying about like beavers, toting buckets of water and split timber pieces (from a stack of firewood) and disappearing over the slope. When David ran in for a drink of water, I caught him by his muddy sleeve.

"What in the world are you guys doing?"

He smiled that enigmatic smile now so familiar. "You'll see, Mom."

Finally, days later, David dashed into my room. "Mama! It's ready!" His blue eyes danced with excitement. He grabbed my hand, pulling me from folding laundry, through the hall, out the door, his grin stretching wider and wider. "Wait till you see it!" He continued to tug me up the hill, down the slope, then right to the digging site.

I stopped dead in my tracks. My mouth fell open in wonder.

He looked up at me, beaming with pride. "I made it for Angie."

There before my eyes was a miniature pond. A small bridge of stacked split logs formed a crude ramp, big enough for one to walk right out to the center of the water.

From atop a tall pole on the shallow shore flapped a white banner. Meticulously printed in David's neat handwriting, it read: ANGIE SHILOH POND.

"Well, Mama, what do you think about it?" He gazed expectantly at me.

I was so choked I couldn't say anything. Emotions invaded, pummeled me. Grief, pride, love, admiration . . . shame. How could I have questioned David's depth of love for Angie? I felt like sinking into the marsh and never coming up.

Suddenly, I understood why I'd not been able to talk with him about it: God was telling me to entrust David into his capable hands.

I swallowed audibly and groped for words. "I think it's a very sweet gesture. Angie would be so proud to know that you built this in her honor." Oh, so proud.

Later that night, David called me to his room, and as he dressed for bed, I sat beside him. The warmth of the shared afternoon lingered.

"Mama, you know why I built that pond, don't you?" As he tugged off his sock, I noticed the grubby, calloused little hands.

"I think so, honey, but why don't you tell me anyway."

"Well—I just had to do something, y'know—big." Blue eyes turned up to my face. And that's when I saw the sorrow in their depths. And the dark shadows beneath them.

"She didn't have much of a life, did she?" he asked.

"What do you mean?"

"Eleven years isn't long to live, is it?" He grimaced as he pulled off his other sock. "That's why I couldn't just do a—dime thing. I wanted to do a—a dollar thing." He grew still for a long moment, reflecting solemnly on that. "I think she knows, Mom."

I nodded, too choked to speak, grasping his second-grade logic. Such was his love for his sister.

For at least a month after our talk that night, David carried water daily to Angie's pond, as soft sand rather quickly soaked it up. Of course, I knew this could not continue indefinitely. As his "do something" grief phase ebbed, Angie's little pond eventually dried up. David moved on to yet other healing and acceptance stages.

For months, I allowed the banner and the rough-hewn bridge to remain on our yard's secluded back corner. I couldn't bring myself to part with it. Rain faded the letters and the wood began to crumble but the message remained alive. Time passed and it continued to comfort me.

Late one afternoon, I stood on the ramp in the silence. And then birdsong penetrated my haze, sweetly transporting me to a plane of peace. I knew in that moment that though David's grief was not always visible, his tribute to Angie surpassed all others combined. I knew also that his gift extended to me.

If David could turn loose, so could I. A soft breeze ruffled my hair and drew my damp face upward. I looked beyond the tall pines into frothy white clouds and infinite blue.

I realized this visit to the pond would be my last.

Because I knew what David, with a child's simplicity, already knew: in the Lord, we never truly lose someone we love.

I blew a kiss and whispered, "I love you, Angie." I turned and walked away.

Emily Sue Harvey

REAL CLASS

*T*hree months before I turned forty, on a cold January day, I was driving down the highway returning home from the grocery store. I began to think about just that—the fact that soon, too soon, I would be turning forty. Suddenly my palms dampened and my lower lip began to quiver. It was altogether a terrifying truth and such a leap from what I thought was my perpetual age of twenty-seven.

What's happening to me? I thought, knowing good and well that the answer was that I'm getting older, I'm aging, and it shows. I realized then that as of late I'd been looking at myself in the mirror for a little too long when applying makeup or fixing my hair. I was scrutinizing the wrinkles and the sags. I'd even been pulling up my hairline to see exactly what gravity had done and what surgery could do. As for my hair color, in the past six months it had changed from sahara sand to nude gold to strawberry sunshine as I attempted to find the perfect shade to not only cover my gray but also flatter my less than vibrant skin, all in the hopes of making me look—younger? No. That wasn't enough. I wanted *young.* I wanted to look thoroughly, absolutely, believably *young* again.

My reaction against turning forty was also evident throughout my house. The coffee table, the floor in my office, my nightstand were all littered with fashion and beauty magazines that weren't even age appropriate. But that was the point. I could learn about, then copy, ways to look (young) and what to wear as suggested by ingenues, starlettes, fashion mavens, and hair designers. My

closets and shelves even started to show my obsession in wor-
shiping these material-imagery icons of youth: the minilength
blue velvet jumper, the black-and-gold brocade platform sandals,
the yellow, blue, and green fingernail polish. And when finally I
would pause and see myself in the reflection of a storefront window, or in the rearview mirror in my car, or in the expressions of
my husband or teenage daughter, did I think that I was winning
the battle I'd waged against aging? Was I successful in defying
the truth of how old I really am? No. Besides that, I looked a little ridiculous and felt a little shallow. I was miserable. I was only
pretending to be bathing in the fountain of youth. My momentary consolation was that in this, I know I'm not alone.

Several months after my fortieth birthday, I was in the airport
on the way to my gate when I noticed, out of the corner of my
eye, someone I needed very much to see—a woman, age sixty,
perhaps older, who was the embodiment of style, fitness, poise.
Forget the vestiges of beauty because, even with wrinkles, she
was still stunning. Her hair, long and gray, was streaked with
bold bands of white and worn up in a classic French twist. Her
figure was fit and healthy in size, not emaciated or overexercised
to the point of looking tense and stressed. She wore a soft pink
lipstick, a perfect shade, and all the color that was needed to
bring out her natural skin tone. She was dressed in a crisp white
cotton blouse paired with black slacks, and on her feet she wore
brown flat sandals; her jewelry was simple, a few gold bangles
and diamond stud earrings. At the moment I saw her she became, unknowingly, my mentor to aging. Her image, her per-
sona, shook me out of my age-identity misery. And it wasn't just
how this woman looked on the outside. There was a calmness,
an expression of serenity on her face, that silently bespoke her
wisdom and understanding through life's many experiences. We
can't have that when we're twenty.

I understood that looking back over my shoulder to youth, to
a time that doesn't exist for me anymore, is counterproductive

to my constant evolution as both a human being and a woman. Why look back when I can look forward? So, I'm a little worn around the edges—so are the best books on my bookshelves, so are the labels on the best bottles of wine I've ever tasted.

SARAH HEEKIN REDFIELD

IT'S UP TO ME

I'm a full-time military wife, which means that I move around a lot. In fact, in fifteen years of marriage, I've had twelve addresses. I've never lived in any one house longer than two years.

I remember after we'd been married six years, had completed five moves, and had two children—one four years old and one a newborn I was in a funk! I felt depressed and extremely lonely.

I wore baggy sweats and no makeup, was overweight, out of shape, and unhealthy, and my biggest accomplishment, it seemed, was watching *Sesame Street* every day at the same time. I looked at peeling, faded, government white walls and merely sighed. I had no plants or decorations in the house of any kind. *Why bother?* I thought. *We're going to move again soon, anyway.* I had lost any motivation I had ever possessed. My "Why bother?" attitude permeated my whole life.

One early spring day in South Dakota, with the temperature a degree or two above freezing, I decided, in desperation, to attend a women's gathering at our church. I almost didn't bother, but thought, *What the heck, they've got free day care!* So I bundled up my brood and headed for church to hear a visiting motivational speaker.

I arrived with no expectations and sat near the back in case I wanted to make an early exit. The theme for the speaker's talk was "Bloom where you're planted." *Yeah, right,* I thought as I started to tune out the speaker, *you have to have roots to bloom, and I never get the chance for that. Why bother?*

I squirmed in my seat for several minutes, but her words and phrases began penetrating my weary mind. She spoke of her concern for those of us who were military wives, and acknowledged our hard lot in life. She suddenly had my attention. More than anything else, I guess, I needed a little sympathy. But after a few moments of sympathizing, she began to gently hammer us—we had no right to feel sorry for ourselves; how lucky we were that our husbands even had jobs when so many did not! And whether we were going to live somewhere for two months or twenty years, it was still our responsibility to leave it a better place than we found it, even if that meant just a few sad petunias in the front yard.

I began feeling guilty and ungrateful. I absorbed her message as a flower absorbs sunshine. I needed to change. I needed to learn how to make the best of my life's situation instead of complaining about it. I hadn't gone into this blind, after all. I knew my husband was a military man when I married him; and I had agreed to the lifestyle.

Her final words bore into me like a drill: "Are you going to waste two years here or two years there of the precious few years on this earth that God has granted you? Get out there and make a difference! Bloom where you're planted, which for now is here!"

I knew as I raced out that door that the first place I needed to bloom was in my own home. I hung up pictures and wallpaper borders. I painted walls that I knew in just a short time would have to be painted back to government white. I planted flowers and a small vegetable garden.

As my surroundings brightened, so did my spirit. My attitude changed, and my appearance followed. I became emotionally and physically healthier. With my renewed confidence, I was able to branch outside of my home and start to make a difference in the community where I lived.

To this day, as much as I dislike packing up and leaving friends and familiar surroundings, I eagerly look forward to planting myself again—each time anticipating an even more magnificent bloom than before.

KAREN A. WILSON

JUNKING—A LESSON IN ECONOMICS

I am an amateur everything—*collector, trader, refinisher,* and judge of fine old woods. It is not essential that one be an amateur in order to blow the budget at a junk shop, but it helps.

On a rainy-day trip to a junk barn in New England, I go in search of an old bed for my young son. Nothing fancy required, simply good solid wood that I can refinish at home. Something to give my son's room that rugged, all-boy, country look.

Two myths of the amateur junker must be exploded right up front. First of all, never go bargain hunting in the rain. We of the inexperienced variety always assume that the best bargains are available on miserable days when business is slow and the dealer will let anything go for a song just to make a sale. Wrong! Because foul weather slows the flow of trade, the wily dealer will take only premium prices on bad days. Besides this simple truth of rainy day bargain hunting, you will probably catch pneumonia and your doctor's bill will add even more to your day's expenses.

Then there is the hour or so spent in careful preparation to create the amateur's air of calculated poverty. A complete waste of time! A seasoned junk dealer can spot a well-heeled housewife with a purse full of plastic from a mile down the road. Underneath her ratty jeans and dirty shirt she's wearing expensive perfume. Or she forgot to removed the diamond studs from her ears, a gift from hubby last Valentine's Day. Let's face it, you just can't fool a junk man!

Without bearing these thoughts in mind, I arrive at my destination filled with naive confidence, ready to storm the antiques barn. My mad dash from the car through the rain is another mistake. Now I am a wet, cold bargain hunter dealing with a dry, comfortable junk man. The only thing cold about him is his heart.

I enter the half-lit barn that's crammed to the rafters with other people's leftovers. My passion! The love of my life! The dealer wanders in my direction—casually, no hurry. I assume he's letting me browse at my leisure. Actually, he's sizing me up. Sniffing the air for Chanel No. 5, checking my earlobes for that telltale sparkle.

"Ayah?" he says at length. (That's New England for "Yes," "Maybe," "Nice weather," "How do you do?" or in this case, "Can I help you, lady?")

"Just looking, thanks." (This remark is ludicrous! No one is out in this hurricane just to browse. He knows it, and I know he knows it!)

I try to recover my air of nonchalance, but it's no use. I've spotted what I want. Too quickly, I blurt out, "How much for this old bed?"

He pulls the headboard out from between a dusty console radio and an overstuffed sofa of Eisenhower vintage. He stands back to admire the piece. He scratches his beard, then his bald head. He squints. He caresses the peeling paint.

"Oh, she'll run you upwards of a hundred dollars, if you try to buy her new."

"But how much for this old one?" (Emphasis on the *old*.)

"She's solid maple, you know. Don't make 'em like this anymore. No telling the history you're buying with her. I could probably let her go for fifteen dollars, seeing as how you came out in the rain and all."

Aha, there it is! He knows what I've been thinking, and he's letting me know he knows. At the same time, he's reminding me that I am wet, cold, and shivering inside my scroungy jeans and patched shirt that aren't fooling anyone.

Voice steely, I announce, "I'll give you twelve."

"Nope! Couldn't let her go for that. She's real good wood."

"Good wood in terrible condition," I point out with some indignation. "It will cost me a small fortune to buy all the things I'll need to refinish that wood."

"Wouldn't know about that. Don't sell refinishing stuff. Just sell furniture, and her price is fifteen dollars."

Time to pull out the stops and make a play for sympathy. "Look, can't you let me have the bed for twelve? It's for my little boy. I promised him. He's been sleeping on the bare floor." (His rolling eyes and my twinge of guilt both brand me an inexperienced liar.)

More scratching, more thinking. Finally, "Well, I reckon you can have her for twelve, but she's worth more. Course, you'll be needing springs. Cost you fifteen dollars."

Triumph is delicious, but no need to press my luck by trying to get him down on the rusty old springs as well. He might change his mind about the price of the bed.

My station wagon loaded with my junking treasures, I head for home, humming a happy tune, already mentally stripping the old bedstead to see if it's really maple under its dozen or so coats of paint.

As I'm unloading in the garage—grinning and muttering praise to myself for my ever-growing expertise at bargaining—I notice a price tag on my $15 springs: *$12.*

Outfoxed again!

BECKY LEE WEYRICH

BEYOND FIRST IMPRESSIONS

We weren't bad kids, just the usual type who occasionally forgot to watch what we were doing. Mr. Johnson seemed to see our occasional dashes onto his lawn as a deliberate plan to annoy him. He was always quick to come outside and see what we were up to. Although he was quite a young man, probably in his early thirties, he had a deep frown line between his eyes that gave him a permanent angry look.

During the summer I was five, all the children had measles, pretty much one child after another. But all it involved was the victim spending a few days in bed. I was the last one who caught the bug, and it didn't pass in a few days. Instead, I had complications: first came the pneumonia, and then pleurisy, at a time when penicillin and other antibiotics didn't exist.

I remember a darkened room—day and night—fitful bouts of sleep, cool cloths on my forehead, and periods of time when I didn't know what was happening. During my sleepless nights, my father sat with me, telling stories and drawing cartoon pictures of my germ. When it was decided that I should go to the hospital, the news quickly spread around the neighborhood.

The evening before I was admitted, my mother was surprised when Mr. Johnson knocked at the door. He seemed to be having difficulty getting any words out. He stood there, eyes downcast, drawing circles with the toe of his shoe. It became clear that he was exceptionally shy, and that he'd come to see how I was doing. Mother invited him in, and he began to relax a bit as he talked with my parents. He told them that it seemed so wrong for "a little kid like that" to be so sick. He told my parents that his wife was unable to have children because of her heart condition. "Bothers her a lot," he confided, "but I don't need kids around."

Both my parents went into my room with Mr. Johnson, knowing I'd be startled when I saw him. I remember an initial feeling of horror, wondering how I could have done something wrong when I'd been sick for so long. I learned later that it surprised him to see my look of fear, and how I slipped down under the covers so that only my eyes were showing.

With my parents still there, Mr. Johnson tried making conversation with me, hindered severely by his shyness and the fact that I was too frightened to answer. Slowly, I realized that this man was trying to be friendly, and I began to relax. Conversation soon was going so well that I didn't even notice when my mother and father left the room.

Discussing the visit later that evening, my parents tried to figure out why Mr. Johnson made this obviously difficult gesture. He'd said he didn't care much for kids, and he didn't need them around; and his manner in the past had been cold. Maybe he acted annoyed with the kids to hide his disappointment that he and his wife never would have children of their own. If that was the case, perhaps it was too painful to hear that a little girl he saw frequently was so sick that she might die.

I spent a month in hospital and remember little except the oxygen tent and the needles in my back to drain the fluid from my lungs. Only my mother and father were allowed to visit. Then there was the evening that my parents were outside my room all night, and the doctor, unnaturally solemn, waited with them, checking regularly to see how I was doing. In those days it was called "the crisis": if the patient managed to make it through the night, improvement usually started right away.

When I came home, Mr. Johnson was my first visitor. He

came in carrying a huge box that he put down on the floor near me. Saying that he didn't know what to get for a sick child, my neighbor added that he'd decided a box of toffee suckers might be a good choice.

About two years later, in spite of the risks, Mrs. Johnson had a baby girl. On the day they arrived home with their child, the new parents invited me over and suggested that I sit down. Mrs. Johnson carefully placed the baby on my lap, saying that I could hold her for a while. I'd never held a baby before. I didn't know what to say when the Johnsons said they had named her Anne because it was my middle name.

As time went by, Mr. Johnson liked to spend a lot of time outside with the baby, mainly because neighbors came by to say how lovely she was. Now a doting father, this formerly shy man smiled and chatted quite easily with the neighbors who admired his baby.

Many times I've wondered if things might have been different if one of us kids had tried talking to our cranky neighbor sooner. Would it have changed our first impression?

I had learned to read and print before I was sick, so I sent Mr. Johnson a thank-you note as soon as I recovered. Many years later, he showed it to me . . . he'd kept it because he thought it was special. At that time, I still had trouble pronouncing words, and my writing reflected the way I spoke. The letter—carefully printed—started out, "Sank you for the thuckers."

JUDI CHAPMAN

VIII
BOUNCING BACK

"I do not suggest you leave your forts and your usual coping tools, only that you open the windows and look at new possibilities."

JENNIFER JAMES

ACT AS IF

*O*ne of the greatest lessons I've learned in *my life is* to *act as if* I'm already the person that I long to be. By *acting as if,* I'm already where I want to be, or have what I want to have. I create a tension between what is and what can be. The law of cause and effect will eventually move me where I desire to be.

This concept works in both small and large ways in our lives. When I was a young, recently divorced woman, I had to support two small children. I needed a job that would provide a living wage. Creating a clear picture in my mind of what I wanted, I started to act as if. I dressed as I would dress if I already had such a job (even though I'd just begun to look). I talked as I would talk if I already had such a job. I acted as if. Within two weeks, a friend of mine told me she knew someone who needed a secretary. I interviewed and got the job with no previous experience.

Then I needed a car for the commute. I asked God and acted as if. Two days later, my new employer announced they had a company car that could be used by a car pool (and there were three of us commuting from my town).

Just the beginning . . . I soon became the assistant director, then the executive director, the editor of the trade magazine, the head of the collective bargaining unit, the creator of a new cooperative organizational structure, and the holder of a reputation for being able to do the impossible.

To those who don't know the simple rule *Act as if,* all of this looked impossible—but for me, it's what I chose and God provided. A friend who is a priest once told me to "let go and know there is God." I am constantly surprised by how loving and caring my God is.

Limited thinking is the only thing that can block all the good waiting in store for us. That's why I practice having a bigger belief. I *act as if* and tap into the infinite source of good. He always gives me what I need and desire, and so much more!

SUE DYER

PERFECT TIMING

Most people conduct job hunts. I conducted a home hunt. Having spent over nine years in Vermont, working in jobs that paid little, I decided to choose a new home—in a new city, in a new state, in a new part of the country.

Eighty-five hundred miles and 182 gallons of gas later, I settled on Austin, Texas. Having traveled through much of the United States on my search, I chose the place where folks seemed friendliest. In Austin, strangers made eye contact with me. They smiled, tipped their heads, and said, "Howdy," with that lovely, long Southern drawl. They chatted with me while I waited in elevators or while crossing the streets. I felt like I belonged.

I left my belongings in Vermont, planning to send for them when I got settled. All I took to Austin with me were two suitcases and the promise I could stay with a friend's family for a week or two until I found work. I quickly began my job search.

I sent out business cards and freshly made résumés listing a local mailbox address and the phone number of a voice-mail answering service. A month passed. I joined the Chamber of Commerce and networked at power breakfasts, lunches, and after-hours business events. A second month passed. I volunteered with a city program hoping to network from the inside. A third month passed. I went to business executive lunches, professional organizations, the Women's Chamber of Commerce, women's networking lunches. Four, five, six months passed.

No one understood why I didn't have a job yet. House-sitting provided me with a roof to live under, and my two filled suit-cases and the local Laundromat kept me clothed. I joined the Job Training Partnership Title III program for dislocated workers. After reviewing my presentation and conducting mock inter-views, my job search counselors gave me high scores. Still no job.

More time passed. Friends began blaming me. "You must be doing something wrong," they said. Yet I did everything I could think of—right down to creating affirmation cards that I read morning and night. I meditated, soaked in bubble baths, lit in-cense, and prayed like hell. The lack of employment seemed un-explainable.

Absorbed by my ongoing bad luck, I got a call from my mother one day. Diagnosed with an abdominal aortic aneurysm, she needed immediate emergency surgery. "Can you fly out to be with me?" she pleaded. With nothing to hold me back, I could leave immediately. I stayed with her as she became immersed in the health care system. While she initially seemed to rebound from the surgery, her strength soon began to wane. About three weeks after her operation, she began to refuse food, liquids, and her medication. She didn't seem to recognize me. An infection and high fever worsened her deteriorating health condition. Al-most two months after her surgery, the doctor finally announced that nothing more could be done for her.

In compliance with her living will, I ordered her gastric feeding tube and IV removed. I stayed by her side the whole time. I held her hand, talked to her, sang her songs, and talked about childhood memories. I stroked her hair, put my head in her lap, and told her how much I loved her. I gave her permis-sion to let go and give up her struggle. She died peacefully soon after.

Returning to Texas, I was faced with the loss of my unem-ployment benefits and house-sitting job. Yet, on an act of faith, I decided to make my commitment clear to stay in Austin and signed a lease on my own place to live. Immediately thereafter, I was offered a wonderful, profitable job.

The previous eleven months of searching, trying to force the world to comply with my idea of what would be best for me, had merited nothing. And now I understood. If I'd been working, I never could have left to spend the time nursing and loving my mother. The job I so longed for would have prevented me from participating in the most precious experience of my life.

What I perceived as a curse turned out to be a blessing. While I believed the world to be working against me, it turns out I was provided for all along. I am, and always have been, exactly where I need to be.

MINDY SUE COHEN

MY SPECIAL BRIDGE

*F*ate played a cruel joke in the summer of 1986 and turned everything upside down.

I had been counseling physically and emotionally abused children, setting up educational material for therapists, assisting the American Cancer Society in their outreach program, working with adults who were experiencing anxiety disorders, and preparing to take the exam for my state license as a marriage, family, and child therapist.

Hardworking, happy, and forty-eight, I now had more time for my husband, with our children ready to leave the nest. My thirsty mind and willing heart loved the excitement of learning new things and reaching out into the community to be of service.

Then something happened. I started to get tired. Very tired. *A bug of some kind that will go away,* I thought. As weeks went by, my muscles began to ache, and I could hardly walk. The memory I had always taken for granted began to dim.

I began skipping lunch so I could take a nap. After work, I took another nap. "A really bad flu," I continued to say to my worried family. My self-diagnosis led me to add to my daily routine what had always worked before: vitamins and fresh, homemade vegetable juice.

Instead of getting better after several months of rest, I got worse.

Finally I dragged myself to the doctor, thinking he could prescribe something that would make "this bug" go away.

"You have a severe case of mononucleosis, and worse than that, you test positive for chronic fatigue syndrome," the doctor said, looking at the blood test results. "There isn't anything I can do that will make it better. Just rest. The mono will go away in a few months, but chronic fatigue can take five years to get out of your system; and in some cases, it keeps reccurring for a life-time."

"Five years," I cried. "I can't be this tired and achy for five years. There's too much to do. People depend on me!"

I guess I thought my desire to continue the life I'd been living could change the diagnosis. It didn't. The mono went away in a few months. The chronic fatigue didn't, just like the doctor said.

No matter how much I tried to push to regain my old lifestyle, I ended up frustrated. At the end of the first year, I could barely climb twenty stairs. I'd given up my daily walks in the hills near our home, quit my work at the counseling centers, and stopped going out with friends, except on rare occasions.

When my husband got a temporary job in Germany and wanted the family to go with him, I had to stay home. They offered to get me a wheelchair and push me around. I knew that even a chair on wheels wouldn't give me the strength I needed to travel.

At the end of the second year, I became depressed. The fatigue just kept ebbing and flowing according to its own agenda, not mine. Frustrated, angry, and embarrassed, I questioned what I'd done to deserve this dilemma.

One day I lay in bed crying and feeling very sorry for myself. Tears streamed down my face and into my ears. I wanted my old life back. I missed the vibrant, fast-moving, quick-thinking, inde-pendent woman, mother, and wife that I knew. My whole body heaved with sobs from the pain of my lost self.

With all my tears spent, I didn't have an ounce of energy left to do anything but lie there. Then something happened. I heard someone speak to me.

Slow down. Just slow down, a voice said. I opened my eyes and looked around my empty room. Did I dream that? Am I now going crazy?

"I have slowed down," I whispered, finding myself drawn into dialogue with the mystery. "I'm at a standstill already."

Are you going to let me help you, or just keep doing this alone? the voice gently prodded. I had been doing this alone. Desperately wanting a way to feel better, I asked for help. Unsure of what this help would be, I tried to listen to the voice.

Just go inside, the voice repeated gently, *and tell me what you're feeling.* I didn't know how to do that, but I was willing to try. What did I have to lose? I took a deep breath in, and instead of pushing away from any discomfort inside my body, I began to increase my awareness of it. In doing that, I entered another dimension, a journey unlike anything I'd ever experienced before.

I floated in and out of colors, shapes, and forms. Red, purple, green, and yellow drifted in and out of deep caverns and elongated tubes. Gurgling noises erupted into a passionate symphony. My skin brushed against soft velvet and liquid gold.

Look at your life, the voice said, *your energy.*

Even though my parents died years ago, I suddenly sensed them with me. I reached out to touch my mother's soft face and rubbed my hand across my father's rough beard. I felt their arms around me, their joy in creating me, their hope for my life, and their overpowering love.

I remembered all the mistakes made, things gone wrong within my family. I wanted to push away from this experience, protect myself. But the voice gently persisted, egging me on.

As I let go and allowed more love, I began to reexperience a myriad of joyful past events. Time meant nothing in this other dimension. I was six years old, pushing the merry-go-round on the school playground as fast as I could. Then twenty-six, walking down the aisle in my wedding dress. Age three, calling for my momma to kiss my skinned knee. Age thirty, giving birth to my daughter. Wonderful, delightful moments played like a movie in my mind; and instead of just watching, I relived them.

When I opened my eyes, I felt a surge of energy shoot through me—an electrical charge that made my whole body vibrate. Following that exquisite, divine experience, I became keenly aware of my misuse of the very thing that my illness robbed me of, *energy.*

The less I used energy in unnecessary ways, the more time I had to enjoy the wonders of life: the softness of the ferns growing in my garden, the sounds of the hummingbird drinking from my orange flowers, a coyote singing through the night air, the smells of winter after our last storm, and the sounds of silence.

My life has definitely been turned upside down. Listening to my body is now something I do regularly. It aids me in my writing, acting, counseling, and everything I do.

Tension, fatigue, fear, illness, or just a tightening in the stomach are signals of some kind. When I take time to acknowledge them, rather than push away from these signals, I receive information that is personal and unique for me.

My once devastating illness has become the catalyst for a new, exciting union—one I will never turn away from again. As to a nectar that feeds my soul, I am joined with the infinite wisdom that I call the Great Spirit, God. And I am joyfully along for the ride!

JUDITH MORTON FRASER

OUTSIDE MY COMFORT ZONE

At eighteen years of age, my worst fear—even greater than death—was to stand in front of a group of any size and give a speech. My feeling of vulnerability stemmed from a traumatic experience I'd had as a fifth-grader, when I accompanied our class choir on the piano for the Christmas performance. In a moment of frenzy, I accidentally turned two pages in the song "Little Drummer Boy." I confused everyone and created total chaos. The vivid memory of the choir director running feverishly between his puzzled choir and off-beat accompanist left me mortified, while the audience laughed at my expense. With absolute resolve, I vowed on that day never again to perform onstage.

So fear consumed me when I learned in my junior year that in order to graduate from high school, I had to take a speech class. I signed up "just to get it over with"—and then promptly crossed my name off the class roster.

While still a junior, I wrote a poem as a tribute to the senior class during this time and desperately wanted someone to read it during commencement. Despite the promise that it would be presented, my poem evidently slid into a bottomless round file, never to be shared.

It's those dreams that are dashed and promises that are broken that inspire action. My senior year, I had no choice but to sign up for speech class. Many times that year, my voice cried out, *Help! I've found my audience, but I've lost my voice!* Every speech brought physical and emotional trauma, complete with nausea, a tongue that weighed as heavy as a boulder, and knees that collapsed.

Again, I wrote a poem—an honor to my graduating class. This time I asked to personally present the poem at the graduation ceremony. As I walked onto the stage past a capacity crowd now invisible in the darkness, one light enveloped me at the podium. Once I spoke the first word, the rest flowed with ease. I heard the applause first, then the lights came on to reveal the crowd. At that moment, I knew that even my darkest fears could never overwhelm me again.

Moments of glory are not achieved by staying in our comfort zone. Moments of glory occur when we step outside ourselves and fear shakes hands with freedom.

CANDIS FANCHER

"It seems pretty basic to me. If you want to feel proud of yourself, you've got to do things you can be proud of."
OSEOLA McCARTY

THE CLIFF

I stared up at the cliff in amazement. No one had said anything about rock climbing. This college course was supposed to be an easy A, and a week free from classes, not Survival 101, I thought. There weren't even any bathrooms.

Our instructor pointed to a log leaning on a lip that stuck out about a quarter of the way up. "We'll walk up the log and then get the ropes out for the rest of the way up."

Nope, I thought, *can't do it. I have a medical excuse.*

"She'll never be a tightrope walker," the doctor told my mom after watching me try to walk a straight line. He discovered that the ligaments in my legs were too short. That explained a lot! Certainly my inability to do sports very well. After years of painful exercises for physical therapy, I moved out of the danger zone of spending my life in a wheelchair, but still not quite normal either.

I looked back at the log. The boys in the class were practically running up to the lip. Well, it is a little thicker than a tightrope, but there is no way I could do it with this pack. This same ugly green pack that I'd carefully packed a few days earlier. With some help from my roommate, I'd hunched down and put the thing on and stood up—then fell over backward onto my bed.

"Who's next?" My instructor scrutinized the group. I looked around. Surely there had to be another way. Solid rock met my gaze in every direction, except the way we just came.

"Me, I guess." What choice did I have? Other than living the rest of my life in the desert.

I put my hands on the cliff wall and slowly inched my way forward.

This isn't so bad.

I slid my foot up the log.

I can do this.

I found another hold for my hand.

Even with this ugly . . .

Slide foot up.

. . . green . . .

New handhold.

. . . backpack.

I made it! I let my pack fall to the ground. Now for the other three-fourths of the cliff. I watched as the guys scurried up the cliff. Show-offs. They didn't even need the rope. One by one, my classmates began to disappear over the cliff.

Once again I thought, *Nope. I can't. I've reached my limit. Don't they realize that heights terrify me?*

With no place to hide, I really needed an attitude adjustment. Unfortunately, it was all up to me. I retraced in my mind what I'd already done so far . . . carried a backpack, hiked through a river with sheer cliffs on either side, slipped on mud and fallen into that river, continued when we saw cougar tracks . . . I didn't quit then, and I won't quit now!

I watched as they tied that ugly green backpack to a rope and hauled it over the cliff. All the stuff I needed to survive for the next three and a half days. What choice did I have but to follow that pack?

They strapped me into the halter and clipped the rope on, instructing me where to put my hands and feet. I listened intently, knowing my life depended on it.

I took hold of the cliff, put my hands and feet in position, and did not look down.

I moved one trembling hand forward.

At least I didn't have to wear the pack.

My foot found its mark.

Maybe this is not so impossible.

Nowhere to put my foot.

"Something's not right," my instructor said from below.

No kidding.

Found foothold.

No one said anything . . .

Right hand.

 . . . about rock climbing . . .

Left hand.

 . . . when I signed up for this class.

Another foothold.

There is no way . . .

Left foot.

 . . . I would have paid to go through this torture . . .

Right hand.

 . . . had I known.

"Come over this way," I heard from above. "It'll be easier for us to pull you up from there." My hands found good spots, my feet found ground as they pulled me over the edge.

I made it! I collapsed a few feet away from the edge and looked over the valley. The red sand seemed to shimmer in the light of the hot desert sun. So beautiful. Like a rite of passage. I knew then that I could do just about anything the world thrust upon me. All I had to do was believe in myself. The choice was mine. I'm glad no one had told me that there would be some rock climbing. I might have never come.

JANICE A. SPERRY

A BLESSING IN DISGUISE

At eight years of age, my biggest problem should have been deflecting the names of Bucky Beaver and Nerd as my teeth protruded from my lips, my bangs hung in my eyes, and my bobby socks sagged at my ankles.

But what place do saggy socks have in the mind of a child when your parents sit you down one day after school and tell you, "We aren't your parents"? Thinking I didn't hear them right, they said it again. "We aren't your *real* parents, and you have a sister." I still didn't hear right. (What was wrong with my ears?) When they said I had a sister living across town, the words fell around me like shards of glass hitting the floor at once. The blood drained from my face as my hands went over my ears and I shut my eyes. *Pretend not to hear, to see, and when I take my hands away, it won't be real,* I thought.

As I stared at Mom and Dad, I sensed their tension, and my stomach churned. "We've been meaning to tell you this for some time," Dad said. "You see, we are your foster parents. Your father ran away right after you were born. Your mother had a nervous breakdown and was placed in an institution."

Reality set in quickly. I learned my biological mother had recently made a miraculous recovery, and the state officials' insistence that a meeting be arranged between my sister, my biological mother, and me forced the conversation upon us.

I started thinking of the secrets I'd have to keep. How could I tell people about this other mother and sister? After all, I still lived here with my now "foster" parents. I felt confused and lonely for the first time. I didn't really understand where I belonged anymore. I felt like my world had just turned upside down, and anger set in. Guilt filled some other holes because I felt responsible. I just didn't want to accept this other family into my life.

But above all, I couldn't share my thoughts or feelings with even my best friends. Certainly, they would look at my foster parents differently. Would my friends disown me or feel sorry for me? I didn't talk to my foster parents about my biological mother or sister either. I couldn't make all the pieces fit. With a jumbled mind and a heavy heart, I pretended to be OK while carrying a secret I just couldn't share.

It turned out my new sister, Andi, who was slightly older, had known about me for a few years and wanted to spend time together. After our forced reunion, we began to see each other occasionally when the system made us. But it just didn't seem right. How could she be my sister if we didn't live together? I lived on the north side of Chicago. She lived on the south side. She had curly hair. I had straight hair. She wore jeans, I wore dresses. She knew all about me, and I knew nothing about her. It really didn't seem like we could be friends, let alone sisters. But Andi wouldn't give up on wanting to get to know me.

During my junior year in high school, Andi invited me to visit her at college. Setting my nervousness aside, I thought it was time to show her some respect. For the first time, I shared my secret with one of my best friends, because I didn't want to make the trip alone. To my amazement, she found the whole situation exciting and intriguing, in contrast to my apprehension.

I didn't say much on the ride to Northern Illinois University. Andi hugged me as I got out of the car, and asked, "Can I introduce you as my little sister?" In that moment, everything turned right side up again in my world. I wondered why it had taken me so long to accept Andi into my life. I was finally ready. All my concerns melted away.

Over that weekend, we found out that although we were different in many ways, we had so much in common, especially how we both love to laugh, take risks, and accept people as they are. Even more important, we both had a desire to make a difference in children's lives.

In three days we built a foundation of friendship. I hugged her and thanked her for not giving up on me. Not only did I enjoy being the little sister, I also got to know my wonderful big sister. I really belonged to someone. I didn't feel as lonely anymore having Andi beside me. The anger and guilt subsided as we learned we weren't responsible for being separated. And the confusion took its own course as, together, we learned about our different journeys and made a pact to stay connected in the future. Andi taught me that I didn't have to keep secrets anymore.

We've kept that promise. We take annual vacations—just the two of us. Our biological mother passed away a few years ago, and she left behind a beautiful two-piece ring of intertwined bands. Andi wears one piece and I wear the other, our way of staying close when we're far apart.

Not too long ago, I sent Andi a card and on the front it had two little girls sitting on a seesaw, smiling at each other. It read, "When I think of the closeness we now share . . . I wish we would have known each other when we were kids."

Why is it that the worst things that happen to us are often blessings in disguise? Making up for lost time, we have made Camp To Belong our legacy. For several weeks each summer, Andi and I reunite hundreds of sisters and brothers who are separated in foster homes, so they can spend quality time together.

The children sing by the campfire, share secrets, take pictures, dance, swim, and play. Just hang out being brothers and sisters. For a moment in time, we have an opportunity to create a more perfect world.

LYNN PRICE

IX
CREATING
ABUNDANCE

"Whatever I focus on in my mind, expands. My mind is the most powerful tool I have for creating the life I want."

JODY STEVENSON

ASK FOR WHAT YOU WANT

A*bout fifteen years ago, I attended a meditation* class at my church in New York City, taught by the minister. At the time, I was in dire straits. My husband had recently left me without warning and wasn't providing me any financial support. And adding to the financial strain, I was helping to support my seventy-five-year-old mother, who was living at a Salvation Army residence. In the class, I was learning some spiritual principles of self-care, such as "I am my own first assignment," "Shyness is not a virtue," and "I am a spiritual being living in a spiritual world guided and governed by spiritual law." On one particular Thursday in late October, our instructor gave us a spiritual assignment. We were to pick out a goal that was to be totally achieved by the following Thursday! We were, as she put it, to "prove God now."

I went away from the class convinced that whatever goal I picked would be immediately achieved. I had received faith! By the time I got home, I had already formulated a financial goal for myself. It was as follows: I wanted money for rent, which came to $418, and I wanted $200 toward Christmas expenses, and a few extra dollars to keep my bank account open. My total financial and spiritual goal was $623, to be realized by class time next Thursday.

In the meantime, I had been negotiating with my husband to get some temporary financial support until I could get a full-time job. Although he had a well-paying position with the state, he was refusing to help me. He finally agreed to meet me and discuss the issue on Friday, the day after the faith assignment had been given.

We met at our favorite restaurant in order to keep the discussion as pleasant as possible. Unfortunately, it turned out to be quite unpleasant; but he reluctantly agreed to give me $25 per week. It was hardly enough, but I was too emotionally upset to argue. At the end of the dinner, he reached into his wallet and pulled out a lotto ticket for Saturday's drawing. Sarcastically, as he handed it over, he said, "Maybe you'll win." I angrily stuffed the ticket into my purse and left.

That weekend I became ill with the flu and didn't think about my goal. But when Monday morning rolled around, I remembered it, and in a spirit of complete and total faith, I began to expect the $623 to arrive from somewhere.

Suddenly I remembered the lotto ticket that my husband had given me. I retrieved it from my purse and called the lotto hot line. I couldn't believe my ears. Out of a possible six winning numbers, I had five on my ticket. I then called the special winner's number, and a kind lady confirmed the fantastic news—I was, indeed, a winner!

I rushed to the subway and went downtown to the lotto offices in the World Trade Center to sign my name on the dotted line. That week, five winning numbers paid $622 and change.

Triumphantly, I went back to class the next Thursday and announced to my teacher and the class that I had achieved God now! I had requested $623 and I had received $623. She paused and said to me, "You should have asked for more."

FRANCINE M. STOREY

NO ORDINARY STOCKINGS

On Thanksgiving *several years ago, my two adult* daughters and I were reminiscing about holidays past. Both agreed that their favorite thing about Christmas was their stockings. I was surprised. It wasn't the beautiful tree with the ornaments they had created or I had collected from around the world. It wasn't the special presents they had requested or memories of family and friends. It was the stockings!

Erika, my firstborn, said she had loved taking down her stocking, rushing into her room, and dumping all the contents onto the bed to sort through.

Now, Christmas stockings were fun for me, too. Ordinary was not acceptable—creativity a must. All year, wherever I traveled or shopped, I searched for small but interesting items. There was always a toy or small game, something educational or from another culture, jewelry, a book, personalized pencils, special writing paper, paintbrushes, barrettes, worry dolls from Peru, and special candy. Their favorite was "gelt" (*Geld*), the gold-foiled chocolate coins from Germany.

As I collected the items, I stashed them into a special drawer. When Christmas arrived, the stocking stuffers were ready. After the children finally went to sleep on Christmas Eve, I removed the empty stockings from the fireplace mantel, filled them, and sometimes, because of the weight, had to prop them on the hearth.

Sometime—I'm not sure when—as the girls became women, the tradition stopped. The stockings disappeared to where old stockings go and I gave the girls "adult" gifts. Perhaps my inner child didn't want to play anymore, or perhaps I thought they would think it silly.

Our discussion that Thanksgiving inspired me to renew the tradition they had loved so much. I began collecting again.

A two-inch, pink, heart-shaped bottle of bubbles fastened to a black neck cord. Fun! A lovely silk and cut-velvet scarf. A package of ten miniature lipsticks. Sensuously scented bubble bath. Necklaces suited to their taste. A classical CD. A small carved box from India. Carefully selected books. And then there was the candy, beautifully wrapped marzipan from Germany and a palm-sized round tin containing balls of milk chocolate the size of large BBs.

I felt like an artist creating a collage. This was more fun than I had remembered. I perused the treasures and wondered, *What sort of stocking will hold all this?* Not being creative at sewing, I began checking the stores' holiday items. At last, there they were—two rather Tudor-looking large velvet stockings, elegantly cuffed, with a delicate overall pattern of contrasting beads.

I carefully filled each stocking, small items in the toe graduating to the larger, and topped off with a bright silver-and-gold holographic paper. Perfect!

The new stockings didn't hang over a fireplace. Instead, they had to be securely packed and shipped to arrive on time in distant cities.

While I didn't get to see their faces, I heard the surprise and pleasure in my daughters' voices as they called to thank me for their beautiful stockings. Then I knew—a tradition that good would never end.

LINDA NASH

"If you don't like what you're getting back in life,
take a look at what you're putting out."
ANONYMOUS

ALL I EVER WANTED

Financial Freedom sounded like an interesting class to take. I arrived ready to take charge of my prosperity, but had doubts when the instructor said right off, "We can look to any one relationship in our life as a model for the way we handle all our relationships." This class was about much more than just how I handled money—it was about my mother! Wherever I went, it felt like she showed up. I avoided dealing with my beliefs about her the same way I'd avoided looking closely at my limiting beliefs about money. Now they were both in the same room, and I had no way out.

Five years ago, I held my only daughter, Kelsey, as she took her last breath, just hours after birth. My world disintegrated. There are no words to describe the intensity with which my heart was torn as Kelsey slipped away.

I barely limped along the year following her death—as if in a fog. My mom talked about Kelsey only when I brought her up. She'd say a little about the pain, then make blanket statements about how blessed we were, because "there's always somebody worse off." Her words were like salt in an open wound.

On what would have been Kelsey's first birthday, Mom didn't

call. Sisters and friends sent flowers, cards, and gifts, but each anniversary found Mom silent.

Over time, I began to find a new "normal." I became less reactive to Mom's blanket statements and omissions, but still closely guarded. I was puzzled and mystified by Mom's silence. She should have been sensitive and responsive to my grief. She, of all people, should understand me.

Three years after I lost Kelsey, my only brother, Joe, died of cancer. Mom had quit her job in order to care for him in his home. She rarely left his side during those last months. The way she cared for him and managed every detail amazed me. The toll—both physical and emotional—was heavy, but she never wavered.

When Joe died, Mom and I grieved together, but the relationship I hoped for still didn't develop. I protected my grief, yet knew Mom's world had been shattered too. On Joe's forty-second birthday I had some idea of what she'd be going through. I knew this first anniversary would be especially heart wrenching and thought of calling. It was the right thing to do, but resentment held me back. Bitterness invented reasons not to call, but they seemed flimsy. Then I remembered the lessons from my Financial Freedom class. "Give what you wish to receive. Imagine how you would feel as the receiver—then give it."

I could acknowledge my pain and disappointment, then set them aside and forgive. With new confidence, I dialed Mom's number and left a message. "Hi, Mom, just wanted you to know I'm thinking about you and Joe. I miss him, too." No longer attached to Mom's acknowledgment of my pain, I felt light, free, and in tune with God. I had done the right thing in reaching out to her, no strings attached.

When Mom returned my call, the energy between us felt loving and relaxed. She said mine was the only message, and the support was much needed. We talked about Joe and how we missed him. I told her how I admired the way she cared for him during his illness and thanked her for being with him. Mom said, "Well, I don't think I could have gone through what you went through, Jean. I know Joe was happy with his life and that gives me some comfort, but what you've gone through losing Kelsey is unimaginable to me. I don't know if I could have done it."

Only hours before I'd accepted that these words from the heart would never cross her lips. Mom acknowledged the loneliness of my pain and shared it even though neither of us could fix it. That was all I ever wanted. Peace washed over me as I realized Joe and Kelsey were witnessing this healing.

Once I became willing to see our relationship through new eyes, Mom did, too. The Financial Freedom class taught me money management is only part of the success equation. Generosity of spirit is my true currency.

JEAN QUINN

CREATING A MIRACLE

My intention to move from San Diego back to my birthplace in the Pacific Northwest was more than just a desire—I was determined. What I lacked in financial wisdom and stability, I had in chutzpah. Struggling with debt, I knew starting over wouldn't be easy. But as luck would have it, my new boyfriend had just purchased an old farm in a small town south of Portland. He would be moving there in a couple of months.

As a fitness professional and personal trainer, I booked clients and classes in that area in advance. This allowed me to make my move and set up housekeeping with my boyfriend. Although I paid no rent, I made sure that I covered my debts and living expenses.

The struggle to start over and earn a decent living was not nearly as challenging as the struggle to stay in what eventually became an unfulfilling relationship. Six months after I had moved in, I needed a miracle to earn enough money to straighten out my long-term financial debt—and to move out.

At that time, a local bank was running an extensive media campaign promoting consumer caution in running up debt. The contest caught my eye. It was fairly simple—write one hundred words or less on how to get out of debt. *Well,* I thought, *I'm an expert on how to get into debt. But now I need to be an expert on how to create my own prosperity.* First prize was $10,000, and the second, third, and fourth were $1,000 each.

While I had never entered a contest before, I had a great idea about how to get out of debt that included setting a short- and a long-term goal, meeting with a financial counselor, and avoiding temptation spending. I scribbled rough drafts for the next few weeks and told no one. I didn't own a typewriter or computer, so writing my entry by hand was my only option. Based on my experience in fitness, I created and submitted the "No-Nonsense Debt Diet." I finished it in exactly one hundred neatly printed words and mailed it with one thought: *This is good enough to win something!*

Two weeks went by, and during that time I remember finding pennies everywhere. Each time I did, I affirmed to myself: *An abundance of money that is rightfully mine comes to me in a joyful way.*

One Saturday morning I taught a class at a local health club, and as I was getting dressed, I found a penny in the box of tissues. It was the first time in the two weeks since I mailed the entry that I thought about the contest, and I wondered when the bank would announce the winners. When I went home, I walked into the kitchen and my boyfriend told me I had several messages from a man named Kermit. I couldn't imagine what a guy named for a famous frog would want with me.

"Did he say what he needed?" I asked.

"The man said he was from the bank, and he had good news," my boyfriend reported. I couldn't get to the phone fast enough!

I now have great respect for names like Kermit—for they come bearing great news. Out of 4,274 Oregon entrants, I was the $10,000 grand prize winner!

And what did I do with the money? I followed my own advice: paid my debts and started planning. Eight months later, I moved out and was once again on my own. Today I own my home, am financially stable, and have made long-term investments.

And what did I learn? When I won the $10,000 prize, I initially looked upon it as a miracle. Then I realized I had moved out of poverty thinking and created my own abundance with each action step I took along the way.

BARBARA DALBEY

THE BOOKSTORE MESSENGER

*T*hanks to my upbringing, which took place on three continents, I was introduced to a medley of cultures, philosophies, ideologies, and more than a handful of superstitions. Nannies threatened me with the wrath of Teutonic supergoblins, while a cook assured me I was being watched over by a flock of genuine benign flower fairies no bigger than her thumb. In Shanghai, my amah, who was raised by missionaries, tried to convince me that my guardian angel would never, ever leave my side—flowing robe, golden wings, and all. I liked my amah best.

Decades later, I still had seen nary a goblin, fairy, or angel.

Arriving at the Portland international airport early one morning with ample time before the departure of our flight, my husband and I walked into a bookstore to browse. Just two steps into the store, I was forced to a quick halt by the presence of a U-shaped service counter in the middle of the store, which created two short and narrow aisles that led to the books on display. There were no other entrances or exits. While I ambled off to the left, my husband took the turn to the right. I landed in front of the mysteries and popular fiction displays and went to work. I was looking for something good to read on our long flight.

Every book I pulled off the shelves and quickly replaced advertised the important fact that the work had made the *New York Times* best-seller list for several weeks. I wasn't impressed and mumbled a few words under my breath that came out something like, "Gosh, darn it. Every damn book I pick up has been on some best-seller list, but not one of them can measure up to the good old classics." I returned the gaudy paperback I was inspecting to its place on the shelf and reached for the next volume.

Suddenly a young man stepped out from the back of the row of shelves closest to me and came into my sight. He had a kind, youthful face, dark chocolate eyes, a well-cut head of light brown hair, and was dressed in designer casual straight out of an Armani ad.

"What you said is right," he replied, his face thoughtful. "Most of the books here have won some praise, some award."

"Well," I replied with light sarcasm lacing my voice, "I'm in the publishing business, and I know for a fact that it takes five percent talent and ninety-five percent luck for a book to become a best-seller ninety-nine percent of the time."

A soft smile spread over his face slowly. He stepped closer and laid both hands gently on my upper arms, turning me slightly to face him squarely.

The moment he touched me, a rippling, comforting warmth rose from my toes to my shoulders. Instead of protesting the young man's unconventional behavior and stepping away from this stranger's reach, I found a calmness come over me and I stood riveted to the floor.

"Listen to me," he said in a low and pleasant voice, his impressive, dark eyes taking over time and space. "You don't need luck, you are blessed." He removed his right hand from my left arm, raised his hand, and pointed at me as he slowly repeated his words. "Listen to me." His voice came more forceful and insistent. "Listen! You don't need luck, you are blessed. We are all blessed. Always remember . . . You . . . are . . . blessed!" With that, he pulled his hand away and was about to return to the spot where he had been book browsing.

I was surprised by the calming effect his simple words had on me, and acting on impulse, I stepped around to his side of the shelf. This time, I put out my arms, gave him a big hug, and said, "Thank you. Thank you so much. I'll never forget your words. I'll live by them. You have given me quite a gift."

As I dropped my arms to my side and took one step back, out of the corner of my eye I saw my husband on the narrow aisle approaching the cash register. I quickly turned to him, blocking the access to the left exit aisle, and called out urgently. "Come here for a second, dear, I want you to meet . . ." My voice trailed off in astonishment, for as I reached for the stranger's hand in order to steer him to my husband's side only a few feet away, my hand touched . . . nothing. The young man had disappeared into thin air.

I shook my head in disbelief. He couldn't have left the store in that split second. I would have had to make room in order for him to reach the exit, and my husband blocked the other aisle that led to the terminal. I retraced my steps, looked at the spot where I had stood, and turned the corner to the other side of the bookshelf, where I had hugged the stranger just a heatbeat ago. There was nobody there. I searched the small store with the thoroughness of a forensic team.

I looked high and low, back and forth, knowing all the time that I had just met an angel.

URSULA BACON

FATHER KNOWS BEST

*S*aturday morning was allowance time at our house. At a designated hour, we children lined up at the library door—that heavy oak door at the bottom of the massive staircase in our home—to get our ten cents allowance. We all got the same amount—no matter what our age. This is the scene I remember:

Father, who sat behind a mahogany desk, would give each of us one nickel and five pennies. As soon as we received those coins, we had to return two cents to him because, as he explained it, "In life, you never get to keep your whole salary. Part of it goes for the taxes, mortgage, or such."

Turning around to leave with our eight cents cupped tightly in our hands, we had an option before leaving the room to drop any amount, or nothing, into a makeshift savings bank made out of an orange juice can with a slit on the top. A label on the can read, TO EUROPE. I can remember my strong desire to earn brownie points. Sometimes I would drop in the nickel, hoping Father would see me do it. My brother would often walk by nonchalantly without dropping anything in the can at all. Once I even saw my father stuff a piece of paper in the slot—an IOU— that he said was his own contribution. How I longed to be a grown-up *now*!

Reflecting on allowance time, I believe these are the lessons I learned early on:

- I can't count on Father to support me.
- You don't get to keep everything you get.
- Brownie points are hard to come by.
- Life is not fair. (My brother and I sailed on the same ship to Europe.)

HILDIE SITTIG

> *"Most people shrink their dreams down to the size of their income."*
> Anonymous

FROM ROLLERS TO RICHES

Besides the joy of being a female entrepreneur and president of my own company, I have earned the title of head janitor. I soon realized being in business for myself is a bumpy series of ups and downs. Black ink on the accounting page did not mean I was completely out of the woods. My extra money was spent on upgrading my office equipment, and I ate heaps of noodles and rice until the next check came in.

I had slid on the ice onto my backside countless times while hauling my dilapidated trash cans up and down the hill in front of my house. How could my speaking audiences know that beneath my cool veneer and tailored business suit was a woman who swore at her garbage cans every week?

I remember one day in particular when the Sierra mountain range was being battered beyond belief by snow and high winds. I'd finally had it with those old garbage cans. They were symbolic of my financial predicament. I was fed up with just scraping by financially and sick of sleepless nights worrying over bills. Somewhere along the way, I had bought into a penny-pinching mind-set. I believed I would never have enough money. I was into scarcity thinking. To me, trash cans with wheels signified a self-indulgent extravagance. So, I continued to drag my trash down the hill, grumbling, "When I have new garbage cans, I'll be rich."

It was close to Christmas when my business associate, Jackson, asked, "If you could have anything you wanted for Christmas, what would it be?"

I glanced outside the window at the snow just starting to flurry and quipped, "If the genie came out of the bottle to grant my wish, I would ask for my business to prosper—I want *super-abundance*. So much abundance that I can buy garbage cans with rollers."

"I've listened to you complain about this for so long," Jackson replied. "Why don't you just go out and buy them?"

"I will—when I have enough money. The company is really leveraged right now, and I'm dead broke." (Once again I argued for my limitations!) "But I know, when I'm successful and am making enough money, it will mean I have made it as a business-woman. I'll be rich," I said.

On Christmas morning, beneath my tree and tied with huge red ribbons were two new garbage cans on rollers. The card read:

> *To my dear friend, Madam President and Head Janitor,*
> *Congratulations . . . Magic happens . . . You're rich!*
> > *Jackson*

I chuckled at the card and was thrilled with my gifts, and his message—"You're rich!"—seeped into my being. Over the next year, my business doubled and expanded internationally. Not only am I speaking, but I do television and radio, and I'm an author. The clients are actually searching *me* out.

And even better, I now understand my limited thinking. Until that Christmas, I didn't believe I deserved those trash cans with wheels. The new garbage cans brought me real richness and peace of mind. That special gift from Jackson gave me a whole new way of seeing myself. *I am worth it!* Strangely enough, when I began internalizing that message, other people began believing in me, too!

DONNA HARTLEY

X
AGING WISELY

"To be able to look back upon one's life with satisfaction is to live twice."

ANONYMOUS

EMBRACING DECEMBER

*L*ast week, in accusatory tones, our youngest looked at me and exclaimed, "Mom, you've got gray hairs!" A film of pity washed over her sad face.

"Don't cry for me, oh my Tina," I sang back at her in my best Evita imitation.

I love these senior years. This is the September of my life, and I can come and go pretty much as I wish, so long as hubby's evening meal is prepared. Poor dear, in forty years of marriage, he still cannot make himself a sandwich. I think he may be refrigerator-challenged.

Yes, I can jump into my soon-to-be-paid-for car and spend the entire day searching for the perfect empty-nest house. Without interruption, I can sit on the mountain or laze on the shore. I can dig in my garden, spend hours in the library, and—get senior discounts at every turn.

Bounding little boys and butterfly girls now bring delights, not duties. Packages of energy, they are nonetheless content to sit on our laps, listen to our stories, and receive our hugs. Aptly named, these babies are grand. And what a privilege to have a teenage grandchild seek our advice. How astounding when they heed it.

Oh sure, the spine and joints aren't always in agreement. The waist is a bit thicker, and my face is pruning up considerably, but I am so grateful for the gifts of my autumn—opportunities to experience simple pleasures that, in times past, scurried by unnoticed in the maelstrom of raising children. Leisure time can be shared: a moment to smile, to warmly thank the salesclerk, time to send off that letter praising or chastising a government official. Time to be involved. Time to savor the moments with children, moments occasionally and regretfully ignored years ago. Like autumn fruit, I've mellowed and thrown off old inhibitions to say what I mean . . . with a smile. Now, on a whim, I'm free to dash out to the store, however attired; my inner mirror tells me I look swell. I dare to wear funky hats, dance with my broom, and hug whomever I want. Today I'm Martha Stewart, creating a gâteau or frosting a torte. Tomorrow I may demonstrate at the state capital, a Diana of justice. Or . . . I shall lie on a rock with the sun in my face. Such freedom, to be who I want and do what I wish.

The marriage is different now; passions are somewhat tempered. Big arguments have descended to amused bickering or unimportant annoyances. There's less resistance too; he accepts that I'll never put the cap back on the tube and I know he'll never stop chewing on ice cubes—loudly. Hands held in church, a communion of minds, we anticipate each other's wants, needs, or opinions. We don't speak for hours, contentedly involved in our individual pursuits or thoughts. Together we laugh at our forgetfulness, smile over a little child, and enjoy the birds.

No flashy car, fancy dinners out, or extensive travels; ours is not the affluent senior life, but our tennis shoes shine just as whitely. Our luxury is found in remembrances of hard work done well, of challenges and sorrows met and overcome. We are gratified that we're forever joined, our souls in love, as well as our bodies.

A developing independence is sensed, a natural evolution toward the inevitable period when only one remains. Preparation is needed. If I leave first, I hope he will make his sandwich. If he ascends before me, I'll not be alone; his mark is everywhere—in the redwood arbor created with unspoken affection just for me, and in his old leather chair, preserving forever the shape of his posterior. Yet we take heart in each other's faith, learning to attain acceptance, to love the Creator more than his creation. We strive to grow before we go. For now, this is good.

And so, dear Tina—and other young ones—as you scurry along, struggling to keep pace with the weaver's shuttle, pause to smell a rose . . . to hug a child. Disdain hairspray and enjoy the wind in your hair. Walk in rain and smell the day. Listen to the clouds. Be kind. Keep going through the pain, sorrow, and disappointments, and preserve—with love—your spirit, for shame is surely a waste. I assure you, summer's growth will bring an autumn harvest of freedom, and joy in the fruits of past labor. Be not afraid to reach the pinnacle. The vista is so very grand: to see where you've been, how far you've come, and to be confident of your position in the world.

When I was thirty, I had no clue. If I'd known how much fun, what freedom, would be found in these September years, I would've lied about my age and gotten here sooner. One little secret, though . . . I think, for Tina, I shall dye my hair just a tad and then prepare—as I embrace December—to wear purple.

LYNNE ZIELINSKI

ROADS NOT TAKEN

*L*ast night I thought about my friend Marge. We were introduced by Marge's roommate, Harriet, who felt passion for a boy named Richard and little else. Marge and I would shake our heads with disapproval at the narrowness of her focus. We considered ourselves truly modern women and Harriet a throwback to another era.

Marge kept a camel saddle in her room at school, a true mark of a rebel with a cause. She wanted to make Middle Eastern studies her life's work and dreamed of traveling there after graduation.

She was a born scholar. A's fell into her lap like apples from a tree after a storm, while I had to study and study.

A year older, I finished college before Marge. To celebrate, we took our first plane trip to Florida. I still remember driving through a rainstorm in a rented convertible. We couldn't get the top up so I solved the problem the only way possible: I held an umbrella over her head while she drove, and we giggled like two madwomen.

We were so much a part of each other's lives once. Now, we rarely see each other. Marge lives more in my imagination. She sought out adventures far from her home base in Chicago, changing addresses so often I write her current address and phone number in pencil in my book.

Marge lived in Israel in a kibbutz, studied in Greece and Paris and Rome, worked for a think tank in Washington and a museum in Hawaii. While I, too, traveled to exotic places, Chicago remained my home.

I loved hearing from Marge. Her calls and letters sometimes

made me wonder: *What did she think of my life? Did she feel sorry for me? Whisper to herself, "There but for the grace of God go I"?*

After all, my life was quite different from hers. I'd lived in the same house, married to the same man for over a quarter of a century.

I'd found my own adventures a bit closer to home but nonetheless daunting. Studied classical guitar and yoga and portrait painting. Worked as a teacher, counselor, writer. Campaigned for causes with a passion even our college friend Harriet would envy. Although my lifestyle suited me, I'd often suspected Marge saw my contentment as complacency.

I probably never would've found out what my friend thought of me if she hadn't collapsed from an undetected heart ailment. That's when I learned she envied me. "You've got such stability in your life. You've got a family. You've got houses and cars and all kinds of stuff. I don't own a thing. I never stay in one place long enough." All causes for admiration, from her perspective anyway.

Now Marge has recovered and, once again, is out seeking new adventures because that is what all true adventurers do. And I wait for her next postcard because that is what friends of adventurers do. Although we may feel occasional twinges of regret, neither one of us really wants to change.

I haven't heard from Marge in quite some time. No cause for alarm. She's probably about to shift gears again.

As I snuggle down in front of the fire into my user-friendly armchair with a stack of my favorite travel books and magazines beside me, I give thanks for the soft boundaries of my own life. While Marge's world—like any foreign city—is a wonderful place to visit, I always look forward to returning home again.

MARY SASS

> *"In youth we learn, in age we understand."*
> MARIE VON EBNER-ESCHENBACH

HOW DOES MY GARDEN GROW?

As my husband, Henry, and I boarded the plane for a much-needed vacation to California, my heart was heavy because our youngest teenage daughter had pulled some rebellious antics the evening before. I prayed that she would behave for my parents while we were away.

In spite of all my efforts to have a good time, I just couldn't get her off my mind. While visiting an old Spanish mission, the first thing I noticed was the beautiful garden. Many varieties of trees, plants, and flowers grew in perfect harmony, forming a tranquil and serene setting for me to get in touch with my feelings. For the first time in days, I felt totally at peace, and as I sat on an old wooden bench meditating, I made this analogy:

God had entrusted Henry and me with eight seeds, and we were the appointed gardeners. Like the plants in this garden, each seed had its own personality and had to be cared for individually.

Our oldest son, Chip, was like the giant saguaro cactus, with its arms outstretched toward the sky. He was emotionally sound, self-sufficient, and needed very little care.

Peggy and Kim reminded me of the delicate ground cover, easygoing, low key, spreading themselves out to protect and help others. Mary and Judy were very visible in the brilliant red flowers of the bougainvillea plant. They liked to be noticed, and were involved in all sorts of community activities, the centers of attention.

As I thought about our youngest son, Michael, I had trouble finding a plant that suited his hyper personality. Just then a precious little hummingbird flew by traveling at unbelievable speed, flitting from flower to flower—perpetual motion. Yes, this was Michael. The small shrub with tiny silver leaves blowing ever so gently in the breeze resembled an angel's wings—our own heavenly angel, David Patrick.

But where was Pam? It was then I noticed the rose garden. It was filled with sweetheart roses, tea roses, climbing rosebushes, and many other varieties, all blooming in brilliant colors. At the very back of the garden was a bush covered with heavy thorns and only one small, tightly closed bud. I had found Pam. This one would need extra special care. She would need to be constantly watered, fertilized, and mulched. And from the size of the thorns, would probably require some sharp pruning.

As I marveled at this beautiful garden, I realized it was not trouble free. There would always be insects to nibble away at the foliage and roots. There would be cloudy days, droughts, freezes, heavy rains, and definitely a storm or two. But there's always a calm after the storm, and a rainbow.

Many uninvited guests may appear in my garden from time to time. There may be weeds, a prickly pear, a crown of thorns, or perhaps even a Venus flytrap—ready to snap me up and eat me alive. But I've learned that if I let them grow, side by side, with my other plants, one day they too may bloom and become an important part of my garden.

So, as the scent of the rose lingers on long after being plucked from the bush, may the seeds of understanding, joy, and love that Henry and I sow reap a beautiful garden for all to share.

RUTH ROCKER

"IT" HAPPENED TO ME

Well, "it" had to happen. It happens to a lot of people. Why should I be any different? Why should I like it any better (or less) than they do? What is this big event? In a matter of weeks, I would be having my sixtieth birthday! That's right, the big six-zero, six times ten, two times thirty.

As I recall, turning what some have termed "the big four-oh" was not very traumatic for me—kind of like "I've made it this far and I don't feel any different."

Turning "over the hill," fifty, was yet another story. Oh, I was OK with my new status in life. I received my obligatory AARP (American Association of Retired Persons) membership application—part of the traditional initiation into the early senior citizen set. And I also began to discover some newfound wisdom associated with my introduction into the silver-haired crowd. I found myself thinking, *Been there, done that,* a lot more often than in the past.

I was content until recently, when a couple of my rapier-tongued offspring reminded me, "Mom, you're more than a half century old," in a tone not unlike comparing me (their mother) to being two days older than dirt.

Not wanting to succumb to negative feelings that I had, indeed, been around a long time, I decided to focus on the bright side of being a senior citizen, the most obvious plus being—*I am still here!* After six decades, this old gal is still kicking, and that's an accomplishment in itself.

So now that "it" happened, I'm confronted with what it means. Being sixty does carry with it some responsibilities. You can't sit life out in your rocker.

I have begun to realize that I am the matriarch of the family, the leader of the tribe, the spokeswoman of our clan, and the upbeat one that those in the succeeding generation will hopefully seek out for sage advice. These new responsibilities are exciting and even a bit intimidating.

The trick, as I see it, is how to be a leader when people do not want to be led, a spokeswoman to others who do not wish to be spoken to, and a wisdom keeper when they are not ready to hear the message. So, now that "it" happened to me, I will try to lead when I can and speak when I should—without using my extended status in life for pushing my views on others.

To think it only took me sixty years to learn this!

Some may ask what my thoughts may be at seventy. All I can say is, let me get back to you on that.

KAY P. GIORDANO

TOMMY TRACKS

I *could sit here and feel guilty, but I don't. After all, I* stay home all day and don't "work," so my surroundings should be impeccable, but it's easy to see they are not.

From where I am sitting, I can spot tiny handprints running across the patio glass door to the outside, and a sheet that drapes over two dining room chairs to form a tent for young Indians who have left a potato chip trail behind as they stalked more exciting game. And still I smile, guilt free.

I call the markings "Tommy tracks." Thomas Jared is the youngest of my grandchildren, and that makes him more likely to be blamed for making more messes than the older kids. More subject to leaving Tommy tracks.

Lego blocks planted in my flowerpots, cookies minus cream-filled centers beneath my couch cushions, and Weeble People in Grandpa's boot are the signature of a small person's existence.

I have visited pristine homes with immaculate rooms where children dare not venture. I've sat on the edge of my chair and admired the elegant displays of breakable valuables on glass-topped coffee tables, and I have carefully replumped the pillows to a just-so-fullness when I was ready to leave—making certain no trace of my visit remained—and I have wondered why. Why shouldn't my tracks remain in this person's world to remind them that I have been there?

I hope the Great Keeper of this earth is not opposed to a little clutter because, for now, I plan to leave an obvious path as I move through this life. I want people to remember I was here!

So, as I sit and write while Tommy naps, I do not feel a compulsive, overpowering need to neaten up the place. The tracks merely serve to remind me grandchildren are spending the weekend in our home.

Soon enough, much too soon, they will grow up and away from this house, and then, if I'm so inclined, I can try for the picture-perfect setting. In the meantime, joining Tommy for a nap sounds like a great idea.

RUTH LEE

"I am my own heroine."
MARIE BASHKIRTSEFF

GODDESS EXTRAORDINAIRE

As a shy, quiet only child of parents in the movie industry, I was often left with sitters while my glamorous parents went on location. I was too young to understand that my dad was the stand-in for one of our country's heroes, John Wayne. I felt abandoned and lonely, and waited anxiously for them to return and give me the attention I was craving. A feeling that I didn't measure up persisted into my adult life, affecting my self-confidence in a variety of ways.

After some gentle encouragement from two close friends, I made an appointment to see Linda, a personal growth therapist. Linda invited me to join a group of women who were on a quest to connect deeply with spirit. In the safe circle of this group, I became determined to pry open my heart and search for past places where I failed to give myself credit for being good enough—places that crouched in fear every time a compliment was given.

During the two-hour weekly sessions, Linda occasionally referred to goddesses or the goddess within. I thought, *What kind of woo-woo is this?* I asked Linda what she meant by *goddess.*

"You know, Jill. The feminine, spiritual side of a woman," she explained. That worked for me.

A few months later, I went to Seattle to visit some girlfriends. I proudly announced, "I am a goddess." My pronouncement brought a few odd looks, but by the end of the weekend, we were calling each other "goddess." That word soaked into my being and felt delicious, full, and empowering. What we created in a somewhat whimsical atmosphere that weekend was too good to leave behind, so I carried my goddess energy home with me and felt free at last.

The following Monday at work, I walked into the lunchroom and noticed a coworker eating a salad and reading the paper. "Janet, you are a goddess," I proclaimed. Janet looked bewildered. "You are a goddess," I repeated. "You are magnificent, resplendent, and essential just the way you are."

I'll never forget the transformation that happened right before my eyes. Janet puffed up, flashed a brilliant smile, and said, "Thank you. You made my day." I got it then. My new goddess being wasn't like some crystal Quan Yen who sat around waiting to be fed peeled grapes—I had work to do, helping women feel good about themselves!

And for myself, as a daily reminder of my calling to remind women of who they really are, I had my checks imprinted with *Jill Davis, Goddess,* and have floral calling cards that read *Jill Davis, Goddess Extraordinaire.*

JILL DAVIS

"Research tells us that fourteen out of any ten individuals like chocolate."
SANDRA BOYNTON

CHOCOLATE LOVE

ome families fight over who gets the heirloom silver or the Chippendale sofa when the old folks die. Not ours. After my beloved mother died and my sister and I met to clear out her apartment, our greed focused on one thing: chocolate.

"I dibs the chocolate in the cupboard," I said as I walked in the door.

"Fine. Then I get everything else," Marian said. "Fair trade."

Then we hugged and cried, and I told her about my first chocolate memory. Marian was a baby during World War II when our father was an army chaplain, and I was only four, but I clearly remember the candy. Before Daddy was sent overseas, he would come home from the military store—the PX—with a Hershey bar. Oh luscious, wondrous, glorious chocolate! I savored every morsel, innocently beginning a lifelong obsession. I don't know why my sister developed the same obsession. Maybe she watched my ecstasy and wanted some for herself.

As teenagers we eschewed anything as calorie-laden as chocolate candy, but as adults we regained our senses and took up the obsession again. More than a habit, this was our indulgence when we faced the difficult years of little money and young children, and then divorces and career dilemmas. Through good times and bad, we cemented our sisterhood with chocolate—a shared Hershey bar when we had little, fancy truffles when we felt rich.

My sister had breast cancer two years ago. The cancer spread to the lymph nodes before they found it and put her through the routine: surgery, chemotherapy, radiation, and more surgery. No more candy for her. Her life focused on a careful diet, lots of rest, and light exercise when she could manage it. A teacher by profession, she explained her illness to her ten-year-old grand-nephews and made sure they saw her baldness and the two wigs and a turban perched on stands in her bedroom. She wanted no secrets, she said. All the while she laughed and joked and kept on working as much as she was able. But I worried about her. We all did. I took her to a radiation appointment and sat with her. "You have to get better," I said, watching the powerful liquid course through the tube. "Who else will give me the right chocolates for Christmas?"

In the early fall, just after her final chemo and radiation treatments, Marian and I and several of her dozens of friends walked together in the Race for the Cure. Some twenty thousand women were there, running, walking, jogging, pushing strollers, waving to cheering bystanders, wearing T-shirts in memory of someone who'd died. Many wore pink *Survivor* hats. In previous years I ran. This time I walked with my sister, spunky and smiling in her pink hat. She was weak, and it was slow going. The others soon passed us. "You don't have to finish this," I told her. "You know that's not the point."

"I want to, I want to," she insisted. So we trudged on, the first mile, then the second, and finally headed into the third.

"Marian, are you sure?" I asked anxiously. I looked closely at her. She didn't seem to be forcing herself, or in pain. Just slow.

"I'm sure."

We two were the last to cross the finish line that day, just in front of the ambulance and the volunteers gathering up the posts and ribbons. The remnants of the crowd cheered, and we grinned and waved, but we had one more goal in mind. We headed right for the postrace treat—chocolate!

Since then, the tests show no reappearance of cancer. There's no guarantee it won't return, but my sister *had* cancer. Past tense. Next Christmas I plan to wrap her favorite Frango mints from Marshall Field's in the silk scarf I'm giving her. And in my will there is a special bequest since, as the oldest, I expect I'll be the first to go: *To my beloved sister I leave my treasured glass bead necklace and all the chocolate in the house.*

I know which one she'll enjoy the most.

MARILYN MCFARLANE

XI
BETTER THAN
LAUGHING GAS

"Laughter is by definition healthy."

Doris Lessing

A NOTE FROM HOME

My husband, David, has never been too fond of Kevin. David sarcastically calls Kevin the wonder dog. He often must have muttered to himself, "I wonder why I told Joanna she could have him."

I understand. David is a cat person. Cat people have trouble making the adjustment to a pet that is so exuberantly loving. David preferred his old cat, Tinker, a walking advertisement for overbreeding at its worse. Tinker, a Siamese male, had crossed eyes, a kinked tail, and a herniated abdomen that caused his stomach to drag along the floor. If he didn't get your attention by standing on your face, he'd yowl in your ear or bite you, definitely not the best of his breed.

Yes, old Tinker was a piece of work and a well-loved piece of work at that, until his misbegotten body finally lay down and died in our basement one sad day.

We needed a replacement pet. The house was too quiet.

Then I found Kevin, a frisky bichon frise who looks, for all the world, like a very, very happy little dust mop on legs. Too happy, it seems, for poor David, who prefers pets who ignore him and make him sneeze.

So it only makes sense that taking Kevin to the groomer is not high on David's priority list.

"But, hon, the groomer is on your way to work!" I whined. "It's silly for me to spend half an hour dropping him off when it's on your way."

David scowled. "Come on, dog breath." He set off for the car with Kevin bouncing along beside him.

Fifteen minutes went by. The phone rang.

"Mrs. Slan? Your husband just showed up with Kevin and, uh, we were wondering." The receptionist sounded very nervous. "Do you really want us to give Kevin a frontal lobotomy?"

I corrected David's instructions and hung up, then stomped into my office to strategize. This meant war. My husband had just upped the ante and I meant to get even. I bided my time.

Six weeks passed by. Kevin was once again a dirty shadow of his fluffy, fur-ball self. His cute little blue hair bow hung from his topknot in tatters.

"Come on, David. Puhleeze. Take him to the groomer," I begged. Kevin sat on his bottom and pawed the air prettily.

David looked up from his coffee and snarled, "OK, but this time I want you to write down exactly what you want them to do. I don't even want to have to discuss that mangy cuss with them. Understood?"

I smiled winningly. "Of course, darling."

He tucked my note into the pocket of his suit coat and gave Kevin a yank. "Come on, you poor excuse for a poodle." Kevin followed him joyously into the garage. As they pulled out of the driveway, I saw David hunkering over the steering wheel and Kevin's black button eyes peering out the window, the blue bow bobbing up and down.

At the groomers, David stepped to the counter with assurance, my written instructions in hand. The receptionist cooed over Kevin. "What can we do for you today, Mr. Slan?" David smiled his smug little grin and handed the lady my note.

She began to laugh hysterically. Another groomer took the note from her hand and read it. Now two groomers were in stitches. David's smile was slipping.

"Could we hurry this along? I have to get to work," he snapped.

They laughed harder.

Finally, they showed him the note. I had printed my instructions very neatly: *Bathe the dog. Neuter the husband.*

JOANNA SLAN

FEAST OR FAMINE

When I was a little girl, my mother would never buy orange juice, fresh or frozen. It was one of those foods my budget-conscious Italian parents considered a luxury. We did, however, have an orange tree, and when the oranges came in season, I would sit under the tree with a book and suck on oranges all afternoon. Orange juice had to be squeezed by hand. No automatic juicer, just my wrist and elbow twisting in three-quarter time. Consequently, a glass of orange juice was a very precious thing, to be sipped and savored.

Probably the best thing about holidays when I was growing up was the meals. The holiday meal was a time to eat special foods not available, too scarce, or too time consuming to prepare the rest of the year. Easter meant fresh asparagus and strawberry shortcake. Christmas was ravioli and panettone with espresso.

That's not the case today. I can't think of a single thing that isn't available in some form or another at the supermarket any day of the year. We have food processors and bread makers to make work quick and easy. Just dump in your ingredients and press *start*. What we don't have the time or desire to make, we can buy, ready made.

So Easter has passed and I can't think of anything that was served up that made my mouth water in anticipation like that orange juice of long ago. If you think I'm suggesting that I would willingly give up my food processor and my evening cappuccino (straight out of the machine on my countertop) to get back that orange juice high, think again. What I am saying is with special foods part of every week's menus, I need something else to make holidays special.

Yet in my family, holiday traditions die hard. We still make the holiday meal the focus of the day. In fact, in my family we make the meal the focus of any occasion when we all happen to be together. Where two or more family members, most of whom suffer from overweight, or high blood pressure, or high cholesterol, get together to plan a celebration, the first topic of discussion is what menu we should prepare. We talk about it and plan it in great detail as much in advance as possible, assigning tasks as if someone is going to have to go out and kill the meat or travel by foot to the next town to procure the salad fixings. We plan, shop, and prepare for a week in advance. The meal accomplished, we're up to our elbows in pots, pans, and suds. By evening, our holiday has been reduced to yawning on the sofa.

So two years ago, at Thanksgiving dinner, I made some bold suggestions.

"You know, these holiday dinners are getting to be too much," I venture. "We spend days preparing, a day cleaning up, and twenty minutes eating. It's not worth it."

My parents, whose whole life is food oriented, immediately sense some sort of insurrection. They warily eye their eldest daughter over their fork-speared gnocchi.

"Oh sure! What else are you going to do? We have to eat." My mother was born with a wooden spoon in her hand. There are no alternatives. We must eat. A lot.

"So because we 'have to eat' we need a whole week cooking and cleaning up?"

"What else are you going to do?" she asks again, beginning to sound a little hysterical.

"The idea is to be together, isn't it? We can play games."

"We can still play games after we eat. We still have to eat," my mom insists.

My sister, Cynthia, who loves games of all kinds and hates to cook, likes the idea. "Yeah! We could play Tripoli, or Taboo, or Scattergories. There are lots of games we could play."

I build on her suggestion. "We can all bring something to nibble on . . . hors d'oeuvres, cookies . . ."

"Oh sure!" Now it's my dad talking. "Hors d'oeuvres! That's a meal? Never mind! It's no big deal to fix a meal." My dad has never done more than hold the pot while my mother scrapes it out into a serving platter.

"It is, if you have to prepare it," I argue.

"Well, I suppose we could potluck," my mom says, in the spirit of compromise. "We could all bring something."

"Right!" I agree. "It doesn't have to be a dinner, though."

"I suppose we could do that." She begins to relent. My dad still doesn't like it. He shakes his head and rolls his eyes, but where food preparation is concerned, pot holders' votes don't count anyway.

My sister and I press the point home. "Then none of us would have to work the whole holiday and be exhausted."

My mother thinks on this for a moment. "Then what will we do for Christmas?"

"Well, we could have a variety—cheeses, a vegetable dip, stuff like that. And some cookies."

"Yeah. That's a good idea," she says, getting up to make coffee. My sister and I sneak a look at each other, triumphant.

"I think a little green salad, too," my mother adds from the kitchen. "We need a salad."

Cynthia and I exchange looks again as her voice continues to call out.

"And we have to have meat. I can cook a turkey. That wouldn't be too much. And maybe some ravioli . . ."

LILLIAN QUASCHNICK

I'LL SHOW 'EM

When subscribing to magazines, I give instructions not to sell my name. I keep track of those who do so by subscribing in the names of my two Maitese dogs, Tiffany and Chrissy. When pitch letters come addressed to either one of the dogs, I know that company has bought a list from one of my magazines.

Sometimes, Tiffy (Tiffany) and Chrissy are called by telemarketers. Yesterday the phone rang, and a lady asked to speak to Tiffany Elkin, to which I replied, "Tiffy doesn't like to speak to strangers." The lady indicated that Tiffany's magazine subscription was about to expire and that she needed to talk to her. Being in a somewhat capricious mood, I yelled for Tiffy, who responded with a withering look as if to say, *Not in this life.*

I then relayed to the telemarketer that Tiffy didn't want to speak to her, and could I take a message? Becoming a shade irritated at this point, the lady said, "Please, let me speak to Tiffany so that we can close this matter."

I knew I had to break the news, so I said, "Tiffany is a dog and she does not want to talk to you." The telemarketer barked, "You subscribed to a magazine in your dog's name? That is the most ridiculous thing I've ever heard of. I've never heard of anything like this before!"

I let her ramble a bit further with her tirade, then graciously and quietly said, "Tiffany has overheard this conversation and is quite upset with you, and she says to tell you that she will not be renewing her subscription to *Better Homes and Gardens.*"

The next thing I heard was the guttural sound *arrgh* and the crash of a receiver.

SHIRLEY ELKIN

TOUGH AS NAILS

Decades ago, seventh grade made me uncomfortable. Until yesterday, seventh-graders intimidated me, and seventh-graders with prison sentences left me downright alarmed. Twenty-four hours ago, I had no intention of ever trying to chat it up with a group of them.

"I'm desperate," my friend Debbie wailed into the phone last night. "Can you speak to a group of junior high school girls for me tomorrow?" Every survival instinct in me wanted to shout "No!" but I knew I couldn't turn down a friend who needed help on such short notice. I reluctantly agreed.

"Good," she said. "Now let me tell you a bit about the girls. They are incarcerated by court order, or have parents who can't handle them, and they've ended up at Angel Camp. I must say, this is the roughest group I've come across. No other speaker has ever made it through a presentation to this group without us having to call in the guards."

This would be impossible. If no one else could command their attention, how could—a rotund, gray-haired, and nearsighted grandmother—make a connection? Surely I had nothing in common with this rough group. I couldn't imagine how to begin.

While I was struggling to find something that would link us together, a friend called. "I may not know much about the Bible, but I know junior high girls," she said. "There are four things they're interested in: their hair, their clothes, their nails, and boys." My, was that call divinely sent!

I took inventory. Their hair ... I was pretty sure that my short, gray-streaked, rather windblown look was not the current style among junior high school girls. My rather fluffy body would look absurd in their style of dress. And I hadn't had a boyfriend in years. But I did know nails.

I had for the first time that summer worn artificial, acrylic fingernails. They looked beautiful. Initially staring at them in awe, I wondered why I hadn't done this before. I thanked the manicurist and left. But getting into my car with long fingernails presented a new challenge. I couldn't open the door. My nails might break! I quickly learned the knuckle technique; voilà, the door opened. Once inside, however, I discovered that simple maneuvers like buckling my seat belt and starting my car became major tasks. When I got home and tried to dial the phone, I got some very strange people on the other end. My computer responded as if I were inputting Greek. My nails, while very pretty, were definitely an impediment to accomplishing anything. I felt I should be wearing a big sign across the front and back of me saying: *Warning! Nail-Challenged Person in Vicinity!*

The crowning blow came at the grocery store when I dropped some change. Thinking, *With these nails, no problem!* (will I never learn?) I stooped to pick up the money, only to have it scoot across the floor. Getting down on my hands and knees in that grocery store, I tried to delicately pick up, then scoop up, the pennies and dimes, using my fingernails like shovels. This did not work; I considered donating the change to whoever might be able to pick it up when a gentleman tapped me on the shoulder and said, "I'll get your change for you, ma'am."

As I faced the junior high school girls, I opened with, "How many of you have worn acrylic fingernails?" A majority of hands went up. I then relayed my harrowing experiences with my nails. They laughed. One girl raised her hand and asked, "Did you get a French manicure?" A French manicure? What in the world could that be? I responded, "I have no idea. I didn't know they came in languages!" We laughed and talked for over an hour about our shared experiences. The conversation proved endearing; I touched them and they, in return, touched me.

Now if someone calls me, I can say I know junior high school girls! I've talked with them, I've laughed with them, and I've glimpsed the potential in them despite their circumstances. I know they are interested in more than their hair, their clothes, their nails, and boys. We may have started out talking about beautiful nails, but we wound up talking about the promise and possibilities hidden beneath the hardened armor of what turned out to be some very beautiful girls.

PATSY DOOLEY

WHILE THE MASTER IS AWAY

When we first decided to get a dog, everyone said, "Get a golden retriever. They're such good dogs. So gentle and sweet. They'll jump through hoops to please their masters."

That's how Kai, a beautiful three-month-old retriever, entered our lives. We gave him the unusual Hawaiian name for *ocean* because we got him from a veterinary clinic on Hawaii Kai Drive in Honolulu.

Almost immediately, we discovered everything we'd heard was true! Kai was smart, gentle, and easily trained. In fact, we were amazed at how well the new puppy fit into our family. Oh, I'm not saying everything was idyllic. In the early days, he did the usual annoying things, like puddling on the rug, chewing everything within reach, and decorating the house with garbage. But after a disapproving look and a loud voice, he soon learned these things were unacceptable. From the very first night, we began taking him for walks around the neighborhood, and I was astonished at how well he learned the basic commands of "sit" and "heel."

We've got us a winner here, I thought. Then came *the business trip.* Frank had to go to Thailand for two weeks. While he was gone, I was rudely awakened to the fact that Kai answered to only one master.

And it wasn't me.

On the second day after Frank left, I arrived home from work and went to the back door to let Kai in. I froze, my eyes widening in astonishment.

Either I was hallucinating or snow had fallen in Honolulu since I'd been at work. On closer examination, I wished it had been the miracle of snow. Kai had taken one of my cushions from the patio furniture and systematically shredded it to pieces. Only one, mind you. The other three were in perfect condition.

I made it perfectly clear to Kai that what he'd done was a definite no-no! Taking what was left of the shredded piece of cotton, I shook it in his face and in my most emphatic voice told him it was "bad, baaad" to destroy my cushion. His big brown eyes stared up at me remorsefully. If he could talk, I'm sure he would've said, *I realize now that I did a horrible thing, and I will never, never let it happen again.* As if to emphasize his remorse, he slunk off to his special spot in the hallway where he always goes when he's in trouble. I threw the shreds of cushion into the trash, sure that Kai and I had come to an understanding.

Until the next day. Imagine my surprise when I went to the back door to discover that, lo and behold, it had snowed again!

Cushion number two was no more.

Kai took one look at my bared fangs and hightailed it off to a corner of the backyard, hoping, I'm sure, to make himself invisible. My blood pressure had undoubtedly risen to a point that should have immediately landed me in a hospital bed! Still, humane person that I am, no bodily harm came to our darling golden except that he got his face washed in the remains of the now-mulched cushion.

By this time it had occurred to me that there was a connection between Kai's dire deeds and my husband's absence. OK, so the dog missed Frank. But why did he have to take it out on me and my innocent cushions?

Day three resulted in cushion number three going the way of numbers one and two.

"Why?" I screamed. "What, in particular, do you have against my patio cushions?"

Kai blinked up at me, an innocent and genuinely puzzled look on his face. *Who, me?* he seemed to be saying. *Why, I have nothing against your cushions. What makes you think such a silly thing as that?*

Day four dawned. One more day, I thought, and one more cushion, the last victim awaiting the move of the vicious serial killer. Would it survive the day? Would I survive Frank's business trip? Would Kai survive the maniacal, crazy woman who used to be Frank's wife?

When I arrived home from work, I cautiously made my way to the back door, held my breath, and peered out.

The fourth mangled victim lay on the lawn, its innards scattered over the grass. And in the midst of this debris sat Kai, staring up at me with a happy grin. The only thing missing from this picture of sweet innocence was a shining halo above his lovely golden head.

I developed a tick in my left eye. My hands twisted into claws. My mouth contorted into a grimace. A growl sprang from my throat.

"I'll kill him!"

If it weren't for my two children, who, for some reason, had developed an intense liking for this demon creature masquerading as a family dog, who knows what would've happened?

Leah and Stephen tucked me into bed and placed a damp washcloth on my throbbing head.

"Don't worry, Mom," Steve said. "Dad will be home tomorrow."

I nodded. The tick in my eye was finally beginning to go away.

The next day, I had recovered enough to go to the airport to meet Frank. On the way home, I told him about the little problem we'd had with his dog. He was properly sympathetic, but I could tell he didn't think it was as serious as I was making it out to be.

Kai was delighted to see his master, and vice versa. As the two of them got reacquainted, I stared at my naked patio set. Only a week ago, it had been so pretty.

Soon enough, everything returned to normal. With Frank safely home, Kai settled down and once again became the dog we'd grown to love. But I do hope Frank doesn't go on any more business trips. Not because I've replaced the cushions. I haven't. It's just that I don't know if my nerves can stand the trauma. I'm probably overreacting. After all, there's nothing left in the backyard that he can hurt. Except for the patio set and the lone plumeria tree.

On second thought, Kai really likes to chew on wood. Once he's finished with the tree, what's to stop him from starting in on wrought iron?

CAROLE BELLACERA

SHORN THING

The wind whipped the glass doors of the hair salon shut behind me, and I stepped out onto the sidewalk, hesitating for a second to let people pass before I made a dash for my car.

What's done is done, I counseled myself as I purposely ignored the rearview mirror and put the key in the ignition. My thoughts raced. *How on earth will I explain this postsurgery, head-injury-victim look to the world?*

It was all Cameron Diaz's fault, you see. She posed last year for the cover of *Movieline* magazine with an adorable short haircut, and I wanted to look just like her. I made an appointment just days before I'd be flying to Germany to meet my boyfriend's parents for the first time and attend his high school reunion. I wanted a too-cute-for-words haircut, not to mention one that wouldn't require the use of a hair dryer that might blow up trying to run on 220 volts via adapter plugs.

Appointment day arrived. My hair wasn't quite shoulder length, but it felt heavy, lifeless, and the style was tiresome.

This is going to feel great! Lighter, carefree, I said to myself. After the shampoo, I dabbed the suds from my ears with a towel and handed Michelle, my trusted hair designer, the Diaz photo.

"That's a pretty short cut," she said. I looked at her quizzically. Diaz's hair didn't seem that short to me; it certainly wasn't any Susan Powter look, by far.

"But I think it will look good on you. It's very big in Europe now," she reassured me.

I smiled and nodded. She began. We caught up on each other's lives as she combed out my dripping tresses. The scissors began in earnest as she talked about her boyfriend, who dumped her for a bimbo the month before. Engrossed in her story, I distractedly watched long clumps of hair roll of my smock as she impassionedly related their last night together, when he told her he thought their relationship might be improved if they could—pretty please—just date other people once in a while.

My head was feeling lighter, really light, in fact, but I didn't look too closely into the mirror—didn't want to jinx a good haircut. In twenty minutes it was over.

All through! No need to blow-dry it; just wash and wear, Michelle hummed.

I grimaced (politely) into the mirror. It was just a hair away from a close shave. She caught my distraught face. Trained to make even wicked, ugly stepsisters think that they look lovely for the ball, my salon maven chirped, "You are one of the few people who can wear this style and get away with it."

I got into the car, but couldn't drive home yet. I needed to make plans for my reentrance into the life-goes-on world. I climbed back out and started walking, desperate to come up with a quick excuse, perhaps even an escape. Wait! I could paste surgical gauze to one side and say I had been in an accident. No, too dramatic. OK, a scarf. No, too obvious.

As I walked along and tossed ideas about, I noticed people glancing in my direction, occasionally doing a double take. I swore I heard murmurings that sounded like "Punk rocker" or "Chemo—how unfortunate." My head felt cold. My ears looked large. I hurried back to the car.

Back home, my boyfriend, always aware how easily my self-esteem teeters on the edge, rubbed my head and gave me some cute nickname in German that sounded suspiciously close to "Stubble Top." Over the weeks, the term *heavy petting* suddenly had new meaning as my head became his new favorite body part to run his hands over.

As it turned out, his family liked me in spite of my missing dead-cell appendages. Although, come to think of it, they did seem rather bent on offering to let me borrow woolen hats to protect my head from "zee feery cold wind." It was the month of May.

I saw another photograph of Diaz in an entertainment magazine recently. Magically, her hair was already shoulder length again.

No harm done, really. This disaster saved me a lot money; I didn't need a haircut for a very long time.

KARIN ESTERHAMMER

MORE CHOCOLATE STORIES?

Do you have a short story you want published that fits the spirit of *Chocolate for a Woman's Soul,* or *Chocolate for a Woman's Spirit?* I am planning future editions, using a similar format, that will feature love stories, divine moments, overcoming obstacles, following our intuition, and humorous events that teach us to laugh at ourselves. I am seeking heartwarming stories from one to four pages in length that feed and lift the spirit and encourage us to go for our dreams.

I invite you to join me in these future projects by sending your special story for consideration. If your story is selected, you will be listed as a contributing author and have a biographical paragraph about you included. For more information, or to send a story, please contact

Kay Allenbaugh
P.O. Box 2165
Lake Oswego, Oregon 97035

kay@allenbaugh.com

For more information, please visit my Web site!

http://www.chocolateforwomen.com

CONTRIBUTORS

ANN ALBERS is a traditional Reiki master, a spiritual counselor, instructor, lecturer, and writer. She received her B.S. in electrical engineering from the University of Notre Dame and worked for eight years in the avionics industry before leaving to follow her spiritual calling. She is currently working on her first two books: *Whispers of the Spirit,* an inspiring and deeply human story of her spiritual awakening, and *No More Taboo!,* a powerful work written to help women reclaim their bodies and their souls. (602) 485-1078. <www.VisionsOfHeaven.com>

MELANIE ALLEN is a full-time student and a part-time employee for an advertising company (during the summer, she is at the office full-time and never at school). She is an avid reader, a hopeful writer, and a very grateful woman to have had the opportunity to be involved in such a wonderful undertaking as *Chocolate for a Woman's Spirit.*

URSULA BACON fled Nazi Germany with her parents and spent the next nine years in China. She was interned, along with eighteen thousand other European refugees, by Japanese occupation forces in Shanghai for four years. She emigrated to the United States at the end of World War II. Ursula is married to author Thorn Bacon, and they operate a small publishing house and write books. She is the coauthor of *Savage Shadows* (New Horizon) and the author of *The Nervous Hostess Cookbook,* (BookPartners, 1998). (503) 682-9821

JENNIFER BROWN BANKS is a Chicago-based journalist, poet, and businesswoman. She has been a contributing writer for *Being Single* magazine since 1995, and has self-published three collections of poetry. Her articles, verse, and commentary have appeared in the *Chicago Sun-Times, Being Single* magazine, *Today's Black Woman, Chocolate for a Woman's Heart, Just for Black Men, Today's Chicago Woman, Chicago Defender,* and *Positive Connections.* Banks is the founder of Poets United to Advance the Arts. (773) 509-8018

CAROLE BELLACERA is a writer living in Manassas, Virginia. Her fiction and articles have appeared in over two hundred magazines and newspapers in America and abroad, such as *Woman's World,* the *Star, Endless Vacation,* and the *Washington Post.* Several works of fiction have won awards in contests such as Columbia Pacific University's *CPU Review* prose contest and the *Belletrist Review's* annual short story contest. Her first screenplay, *Border Crossings,* was a finalist at the 1995 Austin Heart of Film Competition. The novel version of *Border Crossings* was published by Forge Books in May 1999. <KaroBella@aol.com> <http://members.aol.com/KaroBella>

TANNIS BENEDICT grew up traveling all over the world as the child of air force parents. She and her husband, Brian Frankish, have a film development and production company, Frankish-Benedict Entertainment, in which they dedicate themselves to stories of the heart. Her writing debut was a two-character play, *Timing Is Everything,* a romantic comedy produced in Los Angeles, where she lives. She also writes screenplays, short stories, and poetry, and has been an actress for over twenty years. Having lost a son in 1996, her faith in God and the power of prayer have blossomed and illuminated her spiritual path. <tannisb@aol.com>

DIANE GONZALES BERTRAND is a writer whose speciality is books that are suitable for family reading. Her recent novels and books from Arte Publico Press (Houston) include *Sweet Fifteen; Lessons of the Game; Alicia's Treasure;* and two bilingual picture books: *Slip, Slurp, Soup, Soup/Caldo, Caldo, Caldo* and *Family Familia.* She teaches at St. Mary's University in San Antonio, Texas, where she lives with her husband, Nick, and their two children.

C. YVONNE BROWN owns Better Communications in the Workplace. She is a trainer, retreat leader, consultant, and keynote speaker. She offers communication workshops, Humor in the Workplace seminars, self-growth/motivation seminars, and Joy in Life workshops. She uses one of her best-loved tools—humor. She finds humor to be a positive choice in the experience of life and finds real joy in making life more fun for herself and others. (503) 848-8630

KIM CHAMPION lives in Phoenix, Arizona, with her husband, Wayne, and her two teenage sons, Adam and Jonathan. She writes poetry, comedy, and parody and has been writing personalized poetry for over twenty years under the name Poetics Unlimited. She is a ventriloquist (thanks to the inspiration and kindness of Jimmy Nelson). She and her puppet, Stanley, have performed at hospitals, nursing homes, schools, and private parties. She dreams of someday writing a best-seller. <Bergen2123@aol.com>

LOLLY CHAMPION works on legislation for women's health care, participates in Department of Defense breast cancer research programs as a peer reviewer, and sits on various related boards, following her diagnosis of breast cancer. Her mission is to change outcomes for women fighting (and yet to fight) breast cancer. Her greatest joy is teaching her courses, Myths and Realities of Breast Cancer and Being Assertive in Your Health Care, and speaking to business, civic, and community groups about the benefits of early detection. For more information about what you and your community can do to fight breast cancer, call her at (541) 382-9263. <champ@empnet.com>

JUDI CHAPMAN, M.A. is a freelance writer living in Edmonton, Alberta, Canada. She has worked as a university lecturer and as an administrative assistant. <jchapman@edmc.net>

MINDY SUE COHEN describes herself as a "Renaissance woman ever evolving." Her "portfolio career" has required organizational expertise and finely tuned people skills. She's passionate about environmental concerns, is an avid gardner, a chaos tamer, cooking coach, photographer, creative idea generator, problem solver, writer, and home owner. (512) 990-0294

COURTNEY S. wishes to remain anonymous. Her story was written for her by Michele Wallace Campanelli. <mcampanelli@juno.com>

BARBARA DALBEY has been a fitness professional for over twelve years. Her passion for teaching has expanded to include corporate employee programs for wellness and self-image. Her mission is to reeducate and to explore the fallacy of the word *diet* as she focuses on mind, body, and spirit. She enjoys reaching out to people through her teaching, lectures, and articles. (503) 452-7576. <bdalbey@teleport.com>

JILL DAVIS recently retired from office life as the assistant to the president of an HMO. She has since devoted her free time to writing poetry (her favorite poem was published in a chapbook), essays, and a children's book (which she is trying to get published). Born on Catalina Island, she grew up in the Los Angeles area and currently lives in Portland, Oregon. She is dedicating this story to her mother, Norma, her father, Sid, her son, Steve,

her partner, Rod, her friend Jan, and a very special lady, Louise.
<jillz@easystreet.com>

PATSY DOOLEY is an inspirational speaker and author with "the
lighter touch." Her keynotes reflect the challenges of everyday
experiences. Drawing on her twenty-five years in the business
world, she creates funny and value-packed programs on getting
along with people and adding humor to your life. Her gift of
connecting humor with reality brings a fresh originality to her
programs. (940) 592-1009. <Pat2funnyD@aol.com>

SUE DYER is president of OrgMetrics. She works with construction teams who want to prevent or resolve disputes, and
with leaders who want to grow their organizations. She is the
author of *Partner Your Project: Working Together to Bring Your
Project In on Time and on Budget.* She also writes a monthly column, "Dyer Straights," for the construction trade press. She
has developed a reputation as a turnaround expert by transform-
ing troubled organizations into thriving forces. (800) 805-8300.
<SueDyer@orgmet.com>

SHIRLEY ELKIN, M.S.Ed., is a professional speaker and trainer
based in Decatur, Illinois. She presents keynotes, and seminars
on Body Language in the Business World; Change Your Thinking—Change Your Life; and Professional Presentation Skills. She
has worked in secondary education prior to becoming a speaker
and trainer. (217) 875-1721

KARIN ESTERHAMMER is a columnist and editor for the *Los Angeles Times.* She lives in Burbank, California, where her passions
include her two daughters and everything German—language,
culture, history, and cooking. <Karin.esterhammer@latimes.com>

CANDIS FANCHER, M.S. C.C.C., is a speech and language pathologist in a hospital setting. She integrates humor and plea-sure-pausing strategies to enhance patient care, communication, and healing. Faith, family, and friends are her personal highest priorities. She lives with her husband and best friend, Dwayne, a pharmacist, and her children, Chad and Jill, who describe her as being "spontaneously weird." Her Inner Sources seminars, in-cluding Staying Afloat in the Stresspools of Life, entertain, in-form, and inspire participants to stop, notice, act, and create heart-to-heart connections. (612) 890-3897

CAROLINA FERNANDEZ left her job as a stockbroker with Merrill Lynch when she started her family. She now runs a home-based business marketing a line of custom-designed hand-painted children's playwear that bears her name. Hav-ing written her first book on creative motherhood, she is active in a wide variety of writing and public speaking platforms that allow her the opportunity to encourage mothers and inspire their creativity. Her strength and hope stem from a deep and abiding faith in God. She lives with her husband, Ernie, and their four children in Lexington, Kentucky. Visit her Web site at www.carolinafernandez.com. (606) 263-5698

JUDITH MORTON FRASER, M.A., is a marriage, family, and child therapist and an actress. She has published stories, poems, and articles in the *Los Angeles Times* and *Los Angeles Times* syndicate, *Everywoman's Village,* and the California Association of Marriage and Family Therapists newsletters. She is currently writing a novel, *Fiona Lonestar MacLean,* combining creativity, Native American ceremonies, and life passages. She has just completed a screenplay titled *The 50th Anniversary.* Her musical director hus-band, Ian, has won eleven Emmy Awards; daughter Tiffany is an actress; son Neal is a chef; and grandchildren Grace, Chelsea, and Jenna are creative works in progress. (213) 656-9800

MARCI MADSEN FULLER is a writer, wife, and mother, currently living in south Texas with the wild parrots, the water snakes, and the geckos that bob their heads in greeting from the kitchen windowsill. She has just finished her first novel and is now sorting inspirations for her second. (956) 399-3094. <Wlflsprite@aol.com>

JAYNE GARRETT professionally serves as a business/personal coach and facilitator. She writes lyrics, poems, and stories for children and adults. She writes from the heart while interspersing humor into her work. Her greatest joy and inspiration come from her family, friends, and God. <FOCUSunltd@aol.com>

KAY P. GIORDANO resides in Hamilton Top, New Jersey, with her husband of thirty-five years. She lives in close proximity to her seven children and fourteen grandchildren. She enjoys being a thrice-published poet in *Poetic Voices of America*, published annually by Sparrow Grass Poetry Forum. (609) 581-2677

JENNIFER ESPERANTE GUNTER has been an international speaker since 1989. She has spoken in Guam, in Canada, and across the United States. She has produced pregame and half-time shows for the San Francisco 49ers and the Jeep Eagle Bowl in Honolulu. In 1993 she became Miss San Francisco, where she received her nickname "the Cha Cha Queen." She holds a degree in psychology and offers keynotes and workshops for teens and adults, and is a popular mistress of ceremonies. She has appeared on TV and is the author of *Winning with the Right Attitude* and coauthor of *Teen Power* and *PreTeen Power.* (800) 357-6112

GEORGIA C. HARKER is a writer with lifelong interests in the arts and health. She recognizes the profound effect of environment on our mental and physical health. Her writing often focuses on design for health care, art therapy, and other subjects where the arts and health intersect. A jewelry designer for more than twenty years, she is a strong believer in the transformational power of making and incorporating art, pattern, and color into every aspect of our lives. She lives with her entrepreneur/scientist husband and two children. <georgia@cayuse.com>

DONNA HARTLEY is an international speaker, a member of the National Speakers Association, a change specialist, and a survivor of a DC-10 plane crash. Owner and founder of Hartley International, she has been featured on NBC, ABC, PBS, the Learning Channel, and in the *New York Times*. Her popular books, video, and audio training series is called *Get What You Want*. (800) 438-9428

EMILY SUE HARVEY prepared to teach, but the tragic accidental death of her eleven-year-old daughter, Angie, pivoted her in another direction. Writing—begun as therapy—soon became a passion. Those months and years of pouring mind and soul onto paper showed her that disaster need not be the end. Writing focused her on what life *is* and is *not* about. Misfortune taught her to not ask, "Why me?" but rather, "Why *not* me?" Her insights have converged in upbeat stories and novels, both fiction and nonfiction, whose themes ring of triumph in the face of adversity. Her stories have appeared in *Woman's World* and *True Story* magazines. (864) 879-2733. <EmilySue1@aol.com>

ELLEN URBANI HILTEBRAND, M.A., is an author and art therapist who specializes in developing art therapy programs to meet the psychosocial needs of physically ill patients and their families. Her company, Healing Arts, provides national contracting and consulting services to health care organizations. She speaks at medical conferences throughout the country. She served as a Peace Corps volunteer in Guatemala. The therapeutic school art program she developed while there is now used worldwide by Peace Corps volunteers. A book about her experiences in Guatemala should be completed within the next year. (503) 413-8404. <hiltebrand@juno.com>

JENNIFER HOWARD lives in White Salmon, Washington, with her husband and their four sons. She enjoys gardening, horseback riding, and spending time with her family and friends. Writing is a hobby that she uses to capture the milestones in her children's lives. (509) 493-4701

DEBB JANES is a morning radio personality and newswoman in Portland, Oregon. She's also a part-time teacher at Mt. Hood Community College and is working on several books. She's an environmentalist and a lover of the great outdoors. In her spare time, she hikes, climbs, and fly-fishes in the great Northwest. She's also an avid gardener and a believer in self-development through awareness and spirituality. She lives with her thirteen-year-old daughter, Kelsea.

ELIZABETH KRENIK is the mother of three daughters and a twenty-four-year veteran teacher who continually works at understanding that life is a process of learning. She writes a monthly book review column for her local paper and is a public speaker for the Minnesota AIDS Project. She has acted in and directed community theater productions, and currently is writing her first play. (507) 357-6542

CHRISTI KROMMINGA is a freelance writer residing in Monticello, Iowa, where she is an avid chronicler of her family of five, including three children. She especially enjoys recounting the emotions and blessings in the day-to-day celebration of motherhood! (319) 465-5347

RUTH LEE is a grandmother of seven, mother of three, wife of one for forty-four years, and a writer. Her essays, fiction, and poetry have been published by *Evangel, Light and Life Press,* Nazarene Publishing House, and in various regional publications. She is a seven-time first-place award-winning member of the Missouri Writers' Guild. For eight years her column, "A Little Bit of Life," was featured in her hometown newspaper, the *Drexel Star,* where she is still on staff as a writer. She lives in the same small Missouri town where she was born, and considers her writing ability to be a God-given talent. She believes a talent hidden in the ground profits no one. <ruthlee2@casstel.net>

JEANNE EVANS LODWICK, a former gymnastics and ski instructor, now teaches fourth grade. She and her husband and four sons recently moved into their family-built four-thousand-square-foot log home in the woods. She lives in Steamboat Springs, Colorado. (970) 879-2288

JILL LYNNE, a photographer and writer, is known internationally for her special portraits of VIPs, documentation of popular culture, environmental nature studies, use of cutting-edge technology, and alternative photographic techniques. With more than twenty solo exhibitions, her photography is represented in prestigious collections, and her photography and writing have appeared in *Newsweek, Vogue Italia, Ms.,* and the *Miami Herald.* Based in New York City and Miami, she also produces special promotional and fund-raising events for such organizations as the United Nations, the Nature Conservancy, and the American Foundation for AIDS Research. (212) 741-2409 or (305) 532-8096

JUDITH MCCLURE is the director and resident minister of the Center for Expanding Consciousness in Phoenix, Arizona. She, along with her dog, Bear, and cat, Angel, is the official welcoming committee for Sunday services and the many classes held at the center. She teaches Speaking and Creating with Your Angels and Making Unique Water Fountains for Your Spiritual Garden. (602) 279-3998. <j_mcclure@earthlink.net>

CLAUDIA MCCORMICK, a weekly columnist for a metropolitan newspaper for the past ten years, is a former legislative aide to the president of the California Senate and is currently running for public office. She is a world traveler and freelance writer, and is writing a mystery romance novel. She and her husband, Tom, live in Dublin, California, and share a combined family of seven children, eight grandchildren, and four stray cats. (925) 828-1672

ANN MCCOY is a secretary who lives in Vancouver, Washington, with Ed, her husband of thirty years. They have two grown sons and a grandson. She is a beginning writer, who receives encouragement in her efforts from her family and her friend M. J. Evans. <mccoy1969@aol.com>

MARILYN MCFARLANE is a freelance writer and the author of numerous travel books, including *Best Places to Stay in the Pacific Northwest* (five editions); *Best Places to Stay in California* (three editions); *Quick Escapes in the Pacific Northwest;* and *Northwest Discoveries.* Her most recent book is *Sacred Myths: Stories of World Religions,* a vividly illustrated, award-winning book of beloved stories from seven spiritual traditions. She coleads a women's spirituality group and has made pilgrimages to sacred sites around the world. She lives in Portland, Oregon, with her husband, John, and visits her eleven grandchildren as often as possible. <mmcf@easystreet.com>

TERRI MCLEAN lives in northern Minnesota with her husband and four sons. She has been an elementary school teacher in Minnesota and Mexico. She currently enjoys working with students and others in various community activities and is working on stories for children and young adults. <Rlmclean@aol.com>

LAUREN MASER lives in New Zealand and is the director of a marketing and communications consultancy that develops strategies for bringing businesses and their customers closer together. She also presents keynote speeches, seminars, and workshops on motivating teams and individuals in achievement, self-esteem, assertiveness, and developing effective communication skills. Phone and fax: (649) 521-1344. <lmaser@xtra.co.nz>

PHYLLIS MILETICH has been a Sunday feature writer for the *Peninsula Daily News* in Port Angeles, Washington, for twenty-three years. She is the author of three books, *As Seen Through the Ayes of Phyllis Miletich; Understanding It Backwards;* and *Footsteps: One at a Time.* She is a speaker and workshop leader and has written articles for a variety of publications, conducted college writing classes, and worked as a scriptwriter for a Hollywood film production company. She received the top award for nonfiction given by the Washington Press Association's Awards for Excellence, and the prestigious Pacific Northwest Writers' conference, which represents work from five states.

LINDA NASH, M.B.A., is a nationally known speaker, career coach, and author of *Surviving in the Jungle* and *The Shorter Road to Success.* Her practical techniques, enthusiasm, humor, great stories, and motivational style inspire her audiences. She speaks to companies, associations, and organizations on change, communication, personal growth, and career. An ordained interfaith minister, she speaks to church groups and offers spiritual retreats for women. For information on Linda's speaking services, retreats, books, new career workbook, and tape series,

Becoming the Real You and *Getting Paid for It,* call (800) 701-9782.
<Lindaljn@aol.com>

CAROL NEWMAN grew up in southwest Oklahoma among spirited, spiritual women. It is of these women, and for these women, that she writes. A frequent contributor to *Guideposts* and *Angels on Earth* magazines, she now resides in Leawood, Kansas, with her husband, Tom.

MARTHA NICHOLSON is a special needs educator in the field of learning disabilities who provides testing and private tutoring to learning-disabled children and adults. Following an accident, she is home working on her first book, *I Want a Room with a Window,* a recounting of her misadventures at an elementary school. She is also active in crafts and quilting. Her nineteen-year-old son, Brian, also writes. (978) 343-3150

MARIANNA NUNES was a keynote speaker who captivated, motivated, and educated her audience nationwide. She offered programs to Fortune 500 companies, hospitals, universities, and churches in the areas of humor, leadership, and sales training. She was also known for her popular singles program, The Art of Flirting, which was featured in *Life* magazine. After she was diagnosed with cancer, she embarked on a long process of raising her self-esteem and using the healing power of laughter to rebuild her life. Complications with her illness took her life on September 6, 1998, yet her vibrant spirit lives on.

SHEILA O'CONNOR is a freelance writer, newsletter publisher, and syndication agent. Originally from Scotland, Sheila now lives in San Francisco. Her work has been published worldwide and she has placed countless articles overseas for other writers. She has three children, two cats, and three goldfish. When she's not looking after children or pets, Sheila enjoys movies and spending time with friends.

CLARA OLSON is a pastor with a degree in christian education. Her work of ministry to children and families is a model and inspiration internationally. She has written a book for church leaders, *How Do Children Fit into the Meta-Church Model,* and many articles and teacher lessons for volunteers in children's ministries. She is a popular speaker at church growth conferences, women's retreats, and parent training seminars. She is a certified parent effectiveness training (P.E.T.) instructor. Clara is wife to Rod (for thirty-three years) and mom to Cindy and Erik. She is grandmother to Danielle, Brandyn, Tera, Kaleb, and Kaden. (541) 593-6002. <Rod-Olson@msn.com>

MARGARET J. (MIMI) POPP is self-employed and operates a day care center. She lives in Bel Air, Maryland, with her husband of almost thirty years, two wonderful children, their dog, and three cats. She writes personal essays, short stories, and travel articles and hopes to one day find the time to write a novel. She enjoys traveling, reading, writing classes, wine tastings, gourmet meals prepared by her husband, and those rare evenings when everyone is seated at the dinner table. (410) 515-6676. <MIMPOP@AOL.COM>

MARTHA POWERS completed an advanced program in pyschic healing in 1981 and has studied with a great many teachers and healers since that time. She also has a master's degree in library science and uses both disciplines to help connect people with the information that serves them. She lives with God near Portland, Oregon, where she leads workshops for women to balance the chakras, bring in one's essence energy, and be in the holy presence of the angels that bless our lives. (503) 699-7873 <Mpowers@angelfire.com>

LYNN PRICE is founder and executive director of Camp To Belong, a nonprofit volunteer organization dedicated to reuniting siblings placed in different foster homes, for events filled with fun, emotional empowerment, inspiration, and sibling connection. Separated from her sister during childhood, she strives to educate the public and encourage foster and adoptive parents to maintain the sibling bond whenever possible and inspire foster children to take control of their own futures. She serves as a court-appointed special advocate, is a licensed foster parent, and a speaker/writer concerning foster care. She resides with her husband and their three children in Highlands Ranch, Colorado. (303) 791-0915

MARGARET C. PRICE writes novels (*White Violets*), screenplays (*Looking for Mrs. Santa Claus*), and stage plays (*Dove and Dandelion*), when not fixing a peanut butter sandwich for one of her three daughters (Meredith, Julie, and Katie) or chasing after one of her always hungry dogs. A graduate of Northwestern University (in speech) and the University of Kentucky College of Law, she has acted with Actors Theatre of Louisville and advocated children's rights as an attorney. A member of the Writers Guild, she studied film at the American Film Institute and the University of London. She and her husband, Gary, and their family live in Lexington, Kentucky. (606) 263-8131

LILLIAN QUASCHNICK is a former foreign language teacher. Humor is her favorite kind of writing, and she is currently writing about her experience as a first-generation Italian-American. She is also collaborating on a book about the raisin industry. <lmq03@fresno.com>

JESSICA QUILTY is from Quincy, Massachusetts, and is currently a student in Maine working toward her degree in creative writing and women's studies. She is an intern at a small publishing house that specializes in the work of New England poets. She hopes to create literature for young women, and one day open a florist shop.

JEAN QUINN lives with her husband, Mike, and their sons, Brad and Barry. She says that group B strep takes the lives of more newborn babies than any other infectious disease and that anyone interested in preventing unnecessary loss to this common bacteria can visit the Group B Strep Association Web site at groupbstrep.org. She can be reached at <Namaste@aol.com>.

SARAH HEEKIN REDFIELD is the director and founder of the Heekin Group Foundation, a national nonprofit whose purpose is to support the community of new and emerging writers through writing fellowships and educational programs. She is also a freelance writer who frequently publishes articles on topics geared toward educating new writers, as well as essays and short fiction. She is currently working on a book that addresses the genre of creative nonfiction. Hgfh1@aol.com. (541) 548-4147

RUTH ROCKER is a part-time personnel manager and former director of the YMCA Adult Literacy Program in New Orleans. She and her husband, Henry, have seven children, one special angel, and seventeen grandchildren. Christianity is an integral part of her life, and she currently fills the role of Granny for Granny's Angels, a group of youth dedicated to performing Christian service in the community. She recently moved from a large metropolitan area to a small rural community outside the city, where her dream is to pursue her inspirational writings.

JOAN ROELKE is a former banking executive and a freelance writer. She lives in Lake Tahoe, where she is currently working on her second novel. (530) 581-0662

CAROL ANNE RUEL is a writer and communications advisor to the Canadian government. She lives in Ottawa with her daughter Karina, her bearded collie, Zoë, and Kitty, Zoë's archnemesis. In the year since Zoë was freed from a life of severely restricted activity to run like the wind with her lab and retriever buddies, her beautiful face won a photography contest, and she's appeared in a calendar and a Petsmart advertisement. In answer to that distant call from the Scottish highlands, Zoë is currently working on herding certification, much to the dismay of her veterinarians. Her heart is grossly enlarged now, but it continues to rattle away, firing an immense passion for life. <holley@echelon.ca>

MARY SASS, who holds a master's degree in counseling, is a writer, artist, lecturer, and former teacher who has published many essays, short stories, and articles about writing. Her radio scripts and television documentaries have won awards. She has also won awards for her oil paintings, exhibiting in juried one-woman and group shows. She has written novels and illustrated a Christmas novella, *The Katy Ornament*. A member of Mystery Writers of America and the MWA Speakers' Bureau, she is listed in *Who's Who of American Women*, *Who's Who of the Midwest*, and *Who's Who in Entertainment*. (847) 674-7118; from June through September, (616) 432-4466

KAREN SHERIDAN has expertise on the topic of women and money. She encourages and teaches women how to take responsibility for themselves. She is a registered investment advisor, educator, professional speaker, and the author of *Never Take NO for an Answer—One Woman, One Life and the Money Mystique*. She has helped thousands of people explore their relationship with money, and transform it so that they can manifest their dreams. (503) 620-5098. <MakeWealth@aol.com>

HILDIE SITTIG is a freelance writer who majored in zoology, mi-
nored in art history, has a master's degree in education, and has
taught foreign languages for many years. She sells real estate in
southern California. "To die young as late as possible" is her living motto, which creates a positive environment of good living
and healthy eating habits. Born in Germany, she came to the
United States in the early 1930s and continues to travel exten-
sively. Almost resenting the intrusion of mandatory sleep at
night, she cannot wait to experience the fresh newness of tomorrow. (714) 731-6663

JOANNA SLAN is an author, speaker, and contemporary storyteller who inspires audiences of all sizes to reawaken their
sense of wonder by taking a new look at life. She is the author
of *Using Stories and Humor: Grab Your Audience* (Allyn & Bacon)
and *Scrapbook Storytelling* (Writer's Digest Books). For more information, call her at (800) 356-2220; fax (314) 530-7970; E-mail:
<JoannaSlan@aol.com>.

ALAINA SMITH is a writer. Although her jobs have included
newspaper editor, training coordinator, and office manager, writing will always be her primary passion. Hoping to make the transition from writer to author, she is currently working on her first
novel. Her priorities are friendship, family, laughter, and living up
to her personal goals. She is a displaced Oregonian, and currently
lives in Seattle, Washington, with her loving and supportive husband, Frank. (206) 368-9920

JANICE A. SPERRY graduated from Snow College and Westmin-
ster College with honors. She is currently living in Salt Lake City,
Utah, with her husband and her cat.

SHEILA STEPHENS is an international-award-winning poet, writing teacher, columnist, and speaker who enjoys helping people

build their lives "from the inside out." To her, self-esteem is a spiritual journey of accepting the seed of love that divine spirit places in each heart. She's just completed *Light Up Your Dreams with Love;* a poety writing book, *Angels on the Wings of Words;* and several children's books that honor this intent. Her correspondence classes for Write Your Life Stories with Love are also available. <joywriters@uswest.net>

FRANCINE M. STOREY is a poet, playwright, yoga teacher, and member of the Metropolitan Opera wardrobe staff. Her poem "Instructions for Search" can be seen on <www.dinofish.com>. It won the Dylan Thomas Poetry Prize from the New School, New York City, was published in *The Art and Craft of Poetry,* and was made into a short film by Jerome Hamlin, which premiered at the Explorers Club in New York City. She's also published in the *Journal of Irish Literature* and other small press books. She's had numerous productions of her plays performed off-off Broadway. (212) 594-2748

HELEN TAUPE has been a specialist with Behavioral Psychology Services for the province of Manitoba, Canada, for nearly twenty-five years. She currently practices in the city of Winnipeg. One of her passions is writing human interest stories. (204) 452-9767

SUSIE TROCCOLO has recently transitioned from owning a consulting business in the high-tech industry to a new, hybrid life. These days she works two days a week from a home office, two days a week in her organic vegetable garden, and one day a week doing volunteer work with children. Swearing off girl shoes and panty hose, she now walks Rufus and Sassy rain or shine in Portland, Oregon. To celebrate growing older, joy, and change, she has just written a book entitled *Growing Down Stories* as a gift for family and friends. <Auguri@ix.netcom.com>

DOREEN VIRTUE, Ph.D. in psychology, is a lecturer and the author of *The Lightworker's Way*, published by Hay House publishers. She has appeared on Oprah, Leeza, Sally, Ricki, and seventy-five other national and regional talk shows. For information on Dr. Virtue's books, tapes, and seminars, please call (800) 654-5126 ext. 0. <http://www.AngelTherapy.com>

BECKY LEE WEYRICH of St. Simons Island, Georgia, is the author of twenty-five novels, most recently *Swan's Way* and *Savannah Scarlett*. She wrote and illustrated two chapbooks of poetry, and has contributed to five fiction anthologies. She is also a workshop instructor and lecturer. Before turning to fiction in the 1970s, she wrote for a number of newspapers and magazines. A former navy wife, she traveled the world with her pilot husband (now retired) and their two children (now grown). A member of Southeastern Writers Association, Inc., since 1974, she is past president of the organization and continues donating her time and efforts as a member of the SWA board of directors. <beckylw@gate.net>

KAREN A. WILSON is a military wife, mother of two, author, motivational speaker, substitute teacher, self-taught organist/pianist, and Jill of all trades. She holds a bachelor's degree in history and literature from Black Hills State University and is an active member of her church. In fifteen years of marriage, she has had twelve addresses—living and traveling around the world in such exciting places as Italy and South Dakota. Her travels have granted her a wealth of varied experiences. She is currently blooming at Scott Air Force Base, in Illinois. (618) 746-2782

LYNNE ZIELINSKI exuberantly enjoys the friendship of her seven adult children, the magical inspiration of thirteen grandkids, and the loving partnership of her husband of forty-one years. Formerly a nurse, now a business owner, and always a people watcher, Lynne believes life is a gift from God, and what we do with it is our gift to God. She writes accordingly. (205) 880-9052. <Excel11047@aol.com>

ACKNOWLEDGMENTS

My heartfelt thanks go to the contributors of this book. The quality of the relationships we've created in the *Chocolate* sisterhood of women throughout the country and their desire to share unforgettable moments in their lives create the richness found in this spirit-filled book.

Enormous thanks to my agent, Peter Miller; to his staff, Delin Cormeny, Allison Wolcott, and Steven Schattenberg; to my executive editor, Becky Cabaza; to her assistant, Carrie Thornton; and to the Fireside team, for their belief and effort to create a best-selling series.

Major kudos to O. C. O'Connell, Burky Achilles, Ellen Hiltebrand, and Lillian Quaschnick for their editing expertise and their love of *Chocolate*.

My gratitude and deep love to my husband, Eric, who joins me in the desire to grow spiritually as we share our "make a difference in what you do" life together. And as always, my love to friends and family, who continue to support me unconditionally.

The greatest reward from compiling this book has been the awareness of God's presence in this process, and His influence permeates the stories in *Chocolate for a Woman's Spirit*.

ABOUT THE AUTHOR

Kay Allenbaugh is the author of *Chocolate for a Woman's Soul; Chocolate for a Woman's Heart; Chocolate for a Woman's Heart and Soul; Chocolate for a Lover's Heart;* and *Chocolate for a Mother's Heart.* She resides with her husband, Eric Allenbaugh (author of *Wake-Up Calls: You Don't Need to Sleepwalk Through Your Life, Love or Career!*) in Lake Oswego, Oregon.

Look for the
Other Volumes
of Delicious

Chocolate
Stories

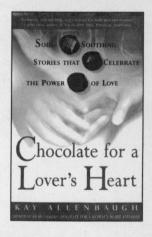